thrift

how to have a stylish home without breaking the bank

KEY PORTER  BOOKS

This edition published by Key Porter Books by
arrangement with Quadrille

2006 Key Porter Books

Text copyright © 2005 by Bridget Bodoano
Design and layout © 2005 Quadrille Publishing Limited

Library and Archives Canada Cataloguing in Publication

Bodoano, Bridget
Thrift: how to have a stylish home without
breaking the bank / Bridget Bodoano; photography by
Graham Atkins Hughes.

Includes index.
ISBN 1-55263-773-5

1. Interior decoration. I. Hughes, Graham Atkins II. Title.

NK2115.B626 2006   747
C2005-906090-5

Key Porter Books Limited
Six Adelaide Street East, Tenth Floor
Toronto, Ontario
Canada M5C 1H6

www.keyporter.com

Printed and bound in China

06 07 08 09 10 5 4 3 2 1

Editorial Director **Jane O'Shea**
Creative Director **Helen Lewis**
Art Director and Designer **Mary Evans**
Project Editor **Lisa Pendreigh**
Photographer **Graham Atkins Hughes**
Picture Researcher **Samantha Rolfe**
Illustrator **Bridget Bodoano**
Production Director **Vincent Smith**
Production Controller **Rebecca Short**

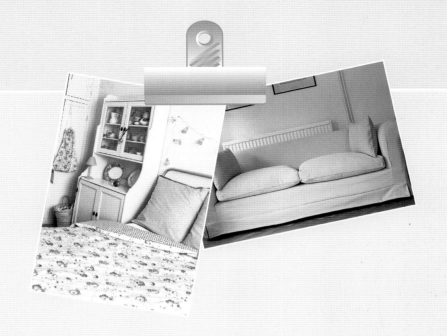

6   introduction

10   thrifty style

32   make the most of what you've got

46   thrifty consumer

72   practical projects

102   frugal fabrics

130   save energy

142   index

144   acknowledgments

introduction

Suddenly, it's smart to be thrifty. For some time, the "fashionistas" have been wearing secondhand clothes, and top designers have been seen scouring thrift shops for garments not only to wear but also to provide them with ideas. Conspicuous consumerism is no longer quite so cool; keeping up with the trends is exhausting, to say nothing of the effect on your bank balance. Prudent people are looking to moderate their desires and, in some cases, change their lives.

Reasons to be thrifty vary from a wish to be stylish on a restricted budget to the rejection of materialism and recognition of the need to cut down for the sake of the planet. Whether you are strapped for cash on the way up or downshifting to a simpler existence, a thrifty approach can help to save not only money but time, energy, and possibly your sanity.

Thrift is more than spending less; it is spending wisely. Now this may sound like something your disapproving elders would preach, but in a world where retail has become a leisure activity, it is difficult not to be tempted by all the goodies on sale. We've all, at some time, bought a load of cheap stuff that, if we're honest, turned out to be a waste of money. If you added up the cost of all the items that you have bought and that did not live up to your expectations, you would find that for the same money you could have bought that thing you really coveted but didn't buy because it was too expensive.

Thrift is not about penny-pinching and deprivation; it is about getting the most for your money, using both wit and wisdom and having fun at the same time.

thrifty style

This chapter gives tips not only on keeping up appearances on a small budget, but on investing wisely for long-term benefit. Though interiors are now subject to the vagaries of fashion, you don't have to be a slavish follower—or a big spender— to have a home that shows you are on the fashion ball. Just as it is possible to put together your own style using a mixture of chain-store and designer labels, plus a few choice accessories, applying the same approach to interiors can result in a home that suits you well.

make the most of what you've got

The proliferation of current TV shows and magazines focused on interiors sometimes makes it seem that the only route to a stylish interior is through chucking away everything and carrying out extensive building works. In reality, something as simple and cheap as a coat of paint can achieve quite startling results.

Familiarity with your home and possessions can make you less appreciative of their good points; and often, just for the sake of change, they are replaced with something that is inferior. A horrible carpet can taint an entire house and make you feel that you need to move; simply taking it up to reveal

chic wooden floorboards can make both you and your home look and feel better. Before committing to expensive building works or replacements, take a good look at what you have.

thrifty consumer

With the ever-increasing availability of affordable good design, the difficulty lies not in finding something to purchase but in knowing what to buy. Some items are not always quite the bargain they appear to be, while others can offer astonishingly good value. This chapter provides a guide to the best buys, including purchase, where to shop, and how to make your acquisitions work well.

practical projects

In order to make the most of what you've got, you may have to embark upon a schedule of repairing, reviving, reinvigorating, or reinventing not only your existing possessions but your home, too. First look at the big picture to assess what needs to be done to bring your whole home

up to scratch. Assess your aspirational ideals, and consider any projects and procedures that will enable you to transform the less than ideal into something highly desirable.

frugal fabrics

Draperies and curtains, shades, cushions, throws and upholstery fabrics are not just finishing touches; they have a huge impact on an interior, especially in living rooms and bedrooms.

Whatever types of fabric you favor—solid-colored cotton and linen; thick wool, velvet, and silk; or a decorative mixture of patterned-weave and printed fabrics—the thrifty approach is to use relatively inexpensive fabrics for the background and invest in smaller amounts of luxurious fabrics to play a leading role in the scheme.

Making your own fabric furnishings and accessories will help to save money and need not require great sewing expertise. Besides ideas for curtains, cushions, and throws, this chapter

includes instructions for a baggy chair slipcover—an easy-to-make, not-too-expensive makeover for the good, the bad, and the ugly.

save energy

Thrift extends beyond your pocket to your personal well-being and the environment. The world needs to be thrifty in its use of resources, which are rapidly being depleted in the face of rampant consumerism. Looking at ways of reducing, reusing, and recycling has become a matter of urgency, as well as expediency. Considering the balance of nature, not just that of your bank account, can also have a beneficial effect on your lifestyle; and taking a new look at how you use your own resources could lead to a different way of life altogether.

thrift—what's it all about?

It is easy to reject the concept of thrift, for it conjures up images of worthy frugality and a rigorous regime of making do or going without, but there is much more to it than that. Spending less while still having fun and being stylish is not impossible. In a fast-moving, ever-changing world, economic uncertainty can strike at any time, so even if you have no immediate need to give up your consuming passions, there is no harm in practicing a little prudence and contemplating the wider implications of adopting a thrifty approach to life.

reasons to be thrifty

it's smart

Canny consumers are realizing that high spending isn't essential for high style and are setting, as well as following, trends that include old as the new "new."

it's necessary

Not everyone is in a highly paid job, and for many, money is tight. Likewise, a change of circumstances—the arrival of a new baby or a change of job—can necessitate a bit of belt tightening.

it's good for the world

You don't have to be an ecologist to be aware that we can't continue with the vicious cycle of consuming and throwing away that pervades Western society. It may make the economy go around, but it is not so good for the planet. More and more people are wanting to do their bit by recycling, buying ecofriendly and sustainable products, and considering alternative sources of power.

it's good for you

The pressures of high consumption can have a deleterious effect on both physical and mental health. Avoiding the pressures of "keeping up" helps keep down debt, while downshifting is no longer seen as failure but is acknowledged as a better way of doing things.

it's a question of priorities

Money and time spent on the home means less money and time for other things. Taking a thrifty approach can free up funds for vacations, keeping fit, culture, entertainment, and hobbies. It could also allow you to invest in learning and retraining, which could lead to a better job or just a refocusing of priorities.

thrifty style

The material things in life cost money, but style is free. Smart people achieve stylishness through a combination of prudence and panache to turn mass-produced into mega-chic and secondhand into swish and swanky. With a few rules, plus a dash of imagination, it is possible to create a look that suits you, your home, and your bank balance.

smart tricks less is more

While the more extreme examples of minimalism have been eschewed in favor of practicality and comfort, the legacy of architect Mies van der Rohe's philosophy of "less is more" lives on in a variety of interior styles. Cathartic decluttering exercises have beneficial effects on individuals as well as their homes; the fashion for paring down has introduced a new, simpler feel to our home furnishings and decoration. And what's more, less costs less.

resist temptation

There are so many well-designed, good-looking, inexpensive products available that it is easy to give in to the temptation to buy more than you really need. A visit to the out-of-town furniture store can soon develop into an orgy of buying; decisions on what to purchase are often clouded by the sheer cheapness of the items on offer, resulting in an unruly assemblage of small, disparate objects rather than a more considered and coherent collection. This can lead to a nasty shock at the checkout with the realization that, cheap though the individual items may be, buying a lot also costs a lot more. To avoid inadvertent overspending, have a clear idea of what you need before you go. Make a shopping list, and stick to it. If something is out of stock, don't rush into buying the next best alternative. It is better to place an order and wait for the item that you really want rather than settle for what will "do for now."

space to breathe

Instead of overcrowding a room, give your furniture some space, to allow greater appreciation of its attributes. The new country cottage style is less chintz and coziness and more natural materials and spare furnishings, favoring sparsely occupied rooms that celebrate the inherent character and raw honesty of stone, wood, and metal.

Traditional interiors give precedence to handsome possessions: taking away the distracting competition of less imposing items ensures that the finer pieces stand out against plainer backgrounds. Even those who prefer the exuberance of more exotic interiors are pruning their possessions in order to increase their appreciation of the best of what's left.

patience rewarded

We live in a consumer culture, where saving up to buy something seems quaintly old-fashioned. Today's easy and instant access to credit means you no longer have to sit on orange boxes until you can afford chairs; instead, moving into a new home that is fully furnished down to the last vase has become the rule rather than the exception. While it is understandable to want a home that is comfortable and fully equipped, the practice often involves rushing into decisions and making do with cheaper options, leading to a look that is a result of compromise rather than conviction.

Building up a collection of furniture and furnishings over a number of years can be a positive experience, and every new, carefully chosen item will be considered and appreciated that little bit more. Good design is timeless, and investment in a few high-quality classics makes sound thrift sense, as they will provide a solid basis on which to build. Take time to decide exactly what you want, and if it isn't readily available, be prepared to wait for it to turn up in the store, at a saleroom, or on the Web.

5 stylish shortcuts

Thrift is not only about what's cheap—investing a little more in one item you adore is a better way to spend your money than buying lots of inexpensive things you don't love but feel you ought to have.

For the cost of several budget buys, invest in one beautiful piece that will last and may even appreciate in value.

One or two good-looking items will always look better than a motley assortment of the not-so-nice.

Building a collection slowly over time lessens the likelihood of impulse purchases and mistakes, increasing the quality of your possessions. If in doubt, don't.

When there are fewer objects in a room, more attention is focused on their surroundings. Make sure the backdrop stands up to scrutiny. Plain walls and floors work well, but even if you prefer pattern, keep the space uncluttered, clean, and cared for.

Expand your color search beyond paint charts and swatches. Take ideas and inspiration from a collection of objects.

The colors in this palette include the subtle tones of a glazed pot and delicate shades of a rose. The exuberant cushion complements the wool throws and is tempered by the pale wallpaper. The postcard offers complementary, subdued alternatives.

smart tricks color scheming

Clever and considered use of color can make the prosaic look sophisticated, harmonize a chaotic house, draw together a motley collection of furnishings and, if necessary, detract from the imperfect.

colour code

Chain-store clothes shoppers wear a lot of black because the alternative colors available often look cheap. It's only when you pay more that you get those subtle and unusual colors that look expensive and chic. The same goes for furniture and accessories, but for "black" read "neutral." An inexpensive sofa upholstered in a natural color can either stand alone or merge into the background, but dress it in harsh, bright colors and it will be shown up for what it is.

As with clothes, fashionable colors for interiors can also prove expensive. But, as clever clothes shoppers know, adding a scarf, bag, or belt in a new color can update a classic outfit. Similarly, thrifty decorators can use large expanses of seemingly expensive color in the affordable form of paint, which can turn an ordinary room into an extraordinarily elegant environment.

classy hues

Look to the high-class fashion labels for color inspiration and, if you dare, take your paint charts into the stores to match up the latest shades. Stores often display clothes grouped in families of colors and tones, as well as patterns and textures, so you should be able to find something to suit your taste. Note how the clothes are accessorized with splashes of other colors. Use this information to put together a palette to form the basis of your own interior scheme. You can even take a favorite sweater along to some paint departments and ask them to reproduce the exact color.

For a classy look, choose muted neutrals such as taupe, warm grays, pale gray-greens, and sage green. Instead of unforgiving pure white, think ivory or bone. Avoid primary colors, for cheap versions are rarely good; but if you want bold statements, go for fruity hues such as canteloupe, tangerine, strawberry pink, banana yellow, or a refreshing squeeze of lime.

Reject sugary pastels in favor of colors with a cashmere aura—soft, pale pinks, blues, and greens. If you want dark color, go for charcoal grays, not black, and think rich, deep purples and reds and matte cobalt blues.

elegant accents

If you, or your home, can't cope with too much color, introduce small amounts through accessories such as cushions and throws, objects and pictures, or a single piece of furniture. These color accents not only brighten up a neutral scheme but also help to unify an interior, giving an impression of careful coordination that could run throughout the whole house, as well as just one room. It is possible to integrate an odd chair plus a mirror or picture frame into the scene with a coat of paint in the same color. However, don't overdo the one color accent, as it can look bitty and contrived. Use no more than two distinctive colors, and mix with shades or tones of just one of them.

smart tricks accessorizing

Smart people can transform last year's clothes into this season's look with a few carefully chosen accessories. Likewise, a few well-chosen extras can lift, enhance, or detract from the shortcomings of a dull piece of furniture or the listlessness of a tired room.

shawls and throws

Cozy up with a cashmere throw, or change the mood with a silky fringed shawl. Large throws can cover a multitude of sins and disguise a shabby sofa. Knitted throws and blankets tend to hug furniture snugly and look neater. Avoid the "bedspread" look by using fashionable layers of smaller throws, mixing tones and textures.

cushions

A new cushion cover in this season's colors will demonstrate your sharp eye for what's now and save you the trouble and expense of a complete makeover. Impart a bohemian air to a shabby chair or sofa with brightly colored, embroidered cushions in ethnic fabrics. Regularly laundered cotton and linen covers will make tired and worn upholstery look more appealing. Neat, firm scatter cushions and bolsters will pull together a saggy sofa, just as squashy ones soften up unforgiving upholstery.

art

A stunning piece of art, ceramic, or sculpture will be the focus of attention and add zest to a simply furnished room. Check out new talent at affordable prices at art school degree shows, art fairs, and local galleries, or be brave and hang your own creations or those of your nearest and dearest. If you can't trust your judgment, then opt for good-quality reproductions of the finest art from galleries and museums.

wild life

Sometimes a joyous vase of flowers can do more for a room than any decorating scheme. Save money on paint and furnishings and invest instead in TLC and fresh flowers. Plants keep us in touch with nature and can calm an interior as well as the soul. A tank of fish will fulfill feng shui requirements and soothe overactive minds.

leather

Just as a beautiful, good-quality handbag or belt can make a chain-store suit look a million dollars, a single leather chair, footstool, or even just a cushion will lend an impression of quality to a room. Keep to classic colors: tans, creams, and dark browns all look expensive.

smart tricks wow!

a splash of color

Your home may be perfectly pleasant, but perhaps lacks just a bit of character. If you want a change, why not go mad with color? If your existing furniture and furnishings are plain and simple, go for something vivid. If you are feeling bold, paint the whole room—or the whole house—otherwise adopt the "just one wall" strategy. Whatever you decide, go for a really outrageous color.

collector's items

There's no need to hide your peculiar passions or apologize for any obsessional tendencies. Bring out those quirky collections, and display them with pride. Whether it is stamps, toy robots, coasters, or even shoes, a collection has the potential to be the center of attention and add a touch of "wow!" to a dull room or more restrained environment.

family portrait

Commissioning a family portrait can be expensive, but is a great investment. If funds are low, you could always have a try yourself. Why not scan in a photograph and play around on a computer or photocopier to produce your own version of an Andy Warhol or a Julian Opie? Better still, equip your five-year-old with brushes, paint, and a huge canvas to produce some Abstract Expressionism.

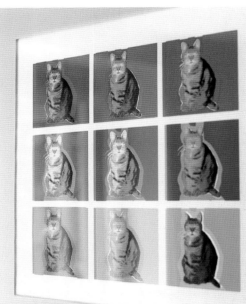

pièce de résistance

If you can't afford to furnish your whole house with the latest designs or most elegant antiques, invest in a single fine piece, and make it the star attraction. Set off simple surroundings with a stunning chair, ornate mirror, or extravagant bed. Put a curious piece of sculpture in the hall or custom-made stained glass in the smallest window. Indulge and enjoy.

smart tricks harmony

Whether you are putting together a home on a shoestring or simply saving money to spend on other things, as a thrifty homemaker you need to be on the lookout for cheap alternatives and bargains. A houseful of inexpensive or secondhand furniture can look a mess unless you impose some sort of order; but it is possible to create a sense of harmony, be it harmony of style, tone or spirit.

style, scale, and proportion

Sticking to one design style to create an Arts and Crafts idyll or a Pop Art pad will naturally pull a room together, but be careful it doesn't look stilted, mannered, or just plain boring. Cheap imitations of design classics often don't cut the mustard, either aesthetically or in terms of quality, so if your taste errs toward the distinctive, invest in the real thing, supplemented with simpler, plainer pieces.

One of the most obvious differences that distinguish inexpensive furnishings from the expensive is scale. Economy solutions often use less material, so proportions are not as generous, and budget buys can end up looking like the poor relations. For example, a cheap sofa or chest can look insignificant next to a more expensive model and detract from an otherwise attractive interior. Economy of scale applies not only to height, width, and depth but also to the thickness of materials used and the size of detailing and fittings, such as knobs and handles.

materials and color

Keeping things simple extends to the materials used for furniture, furnishings, fittings, floors, work surfaces, and equipment. Raw materials, including unpainted wood and stone, and natural fibers, such as cotton, linen, and wool, all have an intrinsically harmonious quality and so work well together to impart a calm feel in a room.

Using too many different materials will look messy, even if they are expensive, so obeying the rules of good design and keeping to a restricted palette is even more important for thrifty interiors.

matching up

Inconsistencies within color and finish can spoil the overall effect of an otherwise good-looking selection of furniture. Wood finishes, particularly on new furniture, can vary widely in color, which is just enough to make them look a mishmash, rather than a carefully chosen collection.

Painting everything the same color, or shades of one color, will unify them, but you can also try toning down the differences with a coat of finishing oil or liquid wax that has a touch of stain in it. Use a limited collection of fabrics to cover a motley assortment of upholstery, and make them look as if they belong together, but avoid an over-conscious, over-coordinated look by choosing a selection of tones, textures, and perhaps a smattering of pattern.

spirit

There is much to be said for a lived-in look, as long as it points to a relatively harmonious life rather than to conflict. A plethora of books and objects and a crowd of furniture can still evoke the spirit of harmony in a happy, cheerful household. All you might need to impose an air of elegance and even opulence in such a setting could be an imaginative arrangement of the furniture, some evidence of tender loving care, or a vase of fresh flowers.

thrifty looks economy modern

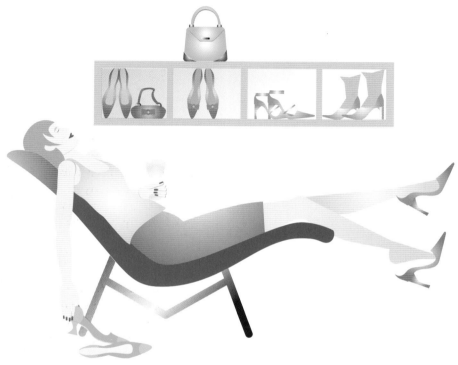

The dictionary definition of "modern" refers to "of the present or recent times" and "fashionable": so in theory, any current design trend can be said to be modern. However, the established concept of "modern" is of simple shapes, clean lines, and pared-down interiors with little or no decoration. The minimalist vision of the perfect white box used to be strictly for architects and purists, but constant exposure in magazines and TV programs following homeowners in pursuit of a "light and airy" space has brought it a wider

currency. However, this form of modernism is extreme, and some people are reacting against it in favor of a more comfortable and characterful look that includes color, curves, pattern, and texture. This shift can be seen in the recent revival and reappraisal of the Scandinavian style, which, with richly colored wood and geometric patterns, has brought in a warmer, less clinical look.

"Modern" is now synonymous with "uncluttered." Thrifty modernists are well advised to keep things simple, but

unless your only activity is quiet meditation and you eat out all the time, you will have a fair amount of stuff to house. Storage is, therefore, an important consideration, in order to keep possessions, equipment, clothes and sundry odds and ends under control, and preferably under cover. "Discretion" and "discipline" are the buzzwords, so put only good-looking objects on display. For everything else, think cabinets with plain fronts that look like part of the wall and melt into the background.

For those who want modern to demonstrate their fashion credentials, it is possible to do it with accessories. It doesn't have to be expensive, huge, or a big statement, it can be something as small and discreet as a single cushion, vase, or picture. Alternatively, you could just casually drape a designer cardigan over the back of a chair, or use your new shoes or handbag as ornaments.

Successful modern looks chic and expensive, and economy modern can be cooked up from inexpensive ingredients picked off the shelves of the large furniture superstores, used sparingly and carefully arranged in a crisp, clean setting.

10 modern issues

keep it simple
Don't overcrowd a room and don't use too many different styles and designs. Stick to simple geometric shapes—the occasional gentle curve is permissible, but absolutely no twiddly decorative trims.

illusion of space
For the must-have "light and airy" feel, use light colors, and choose furniture that is raised above the ground on legs or casters.

hidden storage
Clear away the clutter, and invest in smart built-in storage. Narrow, full-height doors with no horizontal lines to break up the space are very architectural and will also make a low-ceilinged room look and feel higher.

size matters
Keep a sense of proportion and think horizontally. A hodgepodge of different heights will not give you those desirable clean lines.

bare minimum
Keep floors and walls plain. Bare wooden, stone, or tiled floors are great; so is rubber but it is expensive. Paint imperfect floors or cover with plain carpet and rugs.

set the scene
Less furniture looks best, but since it focuses attention on the background, invest money in getting walls, floors, and woodwork into tip-top condition.

color intensity
Control those colors and restrict that palette. Avoid cheap-looking, bright colors and finishes, and go for the sophisticated and subtle.

bare necessities
Keep windows bare, if possible; but if the view, privacy, or cold is an issue, use shades, blinds, shutters, fabric panels, or straight, unfussy draperies.

define and refine
For the crisp look, choose materials such as stainless steel, aluminum, glass, plastics, laminates, and smooth wood with a subtle grain.

see the light
Pay attention to lighting. There are plenty of smart, simple, and surprisingly inexpensive light fixtures around—aluminum and frosted glass are perfect for modern.

thrifty looks delightful dilapidation

Nowadays, secondhand doesn't necessarily mean second rate, especially now that the lived-in look is a fashion statement. Perhaps it is because we live in a fast-track, impersonal age that we currently appreciate old things and find delight in dilapidation. Shabby furniture, peeling walls, and chipped paintwork appear in various guises, ranging from romantic rustic to remembered retro.

Many people enjoy seeing evidence of a past life in an object, believing it adds personality and makes it more precious. This approach is the ultimate in thrifty style, as it encourages you to appreciate your possessions for what they are, rather than what you think they should be, and saves the unnecessary expense of doing things up or buying new.

Over time, garish colors can fade into sophistication, and a bit of battering can be character building, but "shabby chic" isn't always as simple as it may appear. It requires a disciplined and dispassionate eye to distinguish between the potentially delightful and the downright disgusting.

A few rules apply. If something is of good quality and good design, it will probably maintain its dignity when in poor repair. Age rarely gives beauty to something cheap and tawdry or inherently horrible. Cleanliness is also important. Freshly laundered threadbare fabrics are soft and charming, but a shabby sofa or rug can lose its charm if it is accompanied by anything sticky or crusty. The same goes for chipped paintwork, which can look good only if it is thoroughly washed.

It takes flair and a certain amount of courage to take the distressed look all the way. You'll always have the occasional visitor who asks when you are going to get around to decorating, but as long as you maintain order with fewer objects and a willingness to keep things clean and tidy, it is a good option. The uncluttered look works best. Battered objects look more convincing against a freshly painted background. Similarly, if you love your distressed walls, keep the competition to a minimum with fewer, simpler furnishings.

For really small budgets, scrubbed floorboards are infinitely preferable to a hideous carpet, and stripped, washed-down walls much better than ugly wallpaper. When it comes to buying old or antique furnishings and accessories, something in fine condition may be well beyond your pocket, but something in not quite tip-top condition could well be affordable. Assess the damage not only for aesthetic qualities but for practical reasons; an old armchair may look just the thing, but if the springs have gone, it will be uncomfortable and possibly unusable. Repairs can be expensive and tricky; some may even need the attention of an expert, but sometimes patience and basic D.I.Y skills are enough.

Contrast can enhance the charm of the old and the pleasing purity of the new. A coat of paint will smarten up and cover up a certain amount of damage without destroying the character of an old table or chest of drawers, while new seat cushions and covers will make a sofa more comfortable as well as more attractive.

Of course, if is possible to make new look old by using special paint techniques or just by using old fabrics and coverings and traditional colors and finishes on furnishings, walls, and floors. Many new products are now available ready distressed. Some are very successful, but some are not, so be discriminating, and make sure the dilapidation is definitely delightful.

shabby favorites

Old woolen, plaid blankets—look for grungy browns, muted pinks, and greens. Honeycomb and tapestry blankets, much favored in the 1960s and sold in craft shops and woolen mills, are also back in favor.

Crocheted blankets, shawls, and cushion covers—charming and cozy. A crocheted tea cozy completes the effect.

Old patchwork and quilted bedcovers—the more faded the better, and don't worry if the insides are poking through.

Candlewick bedspreads—once considered rather passe but now definitely "now."

Big, saggy armchairs (just one, though, as more can look too scruffy). Leather is special but becoming hard to find at affordable prices.

Faded chintz—look out for draperies, curtains, and sofa and chair covers.

Metal garden furniture, wirework plant holders, and odds and ends. A bit of rust adds character.

Small, painted bookcases and shelves—a nostalgic alternative to smart shelving.

Faded pictures in stout wooden frames, including old sepia photographs (adopt your own ancestors).

thrifty looks natural calm

For many people, the discipline of modernism is very appealing, but it just doesn't suit their lifestyle. However, a comfortable and a more casual environment can still look and feel calm, and applying a few principles of Zen will help. Space, simplicity, order, balance, and harmony are important ingredients, as is a focus on nature.

Though not strictly minimalist, a Zen interior contains only items that are pleasing to the eye and practical. This is a useful rule when decluttering, but since it does not preclude anything a bit battered or slightly out of date, it is a philosophy that will appeal to the thrifty. "Pleasing to the eye" doesn't have to mean design perfect, so the imperfections of much-loved, familiar items are unimportant, because their comforting presence is calming and good for the spirit.

An overcrowded room will seldom feel calm, so consider the space, and leave enough room for moving around and stretching out. Though it may not always be possible to impose calm on family rooms, the philosophy is ideal for bedrooms; for it is acknowledged that we sleep and relax better in an uncluttered environment: the cell-like simplicity of bare floors and walls, the minimum amount of furniture, just a comfortable bed, a bedside table, and a few favorite items.

The chemical-rich, highly charged atmosphere of the technological age is at odds with our origins, and it is not surprising that many people are leaving the towns and opting for country living.

Of those left behind, many more aspire to a simpler life and the beneficial effects of the countryside, including the appreciation of nature. Surrounding ourselves with colors and materials directly derived from nature can help us to reconnect and so become more relaxed and re-energized. Wooden and stone floors are perfect, but wool carpet or natural fiber floor coverings will provide a quieter environment.

Along with color and style, use some of the "harmony" smart tricks to induce an aura of calm with natural tones. Choose vegetable dyes rather than the harsher chemical varieties, solid woods, and shapes that are rounded rather than sharp. Keep it serene by staying simple, with not too much to distract the eye or the brain. Calm doesn't necessarily mean stilted. Taking pleasure in the rituals of everyday actions such as cooking and cleaning is also a tenet of Zen and involves enjoying the beauty of everyday objects such as wooden bowls, simple white ceramics, even a favorite knife and chopping board.

Light is essential for well-being, but a calm atmosphere is created through quality of light, whether it is filtering it through fine cotton curtains or wooden slatted blinds or arranging lamps to provide pools of light, rather than general illumination.

Colors in nature harmonize naturally. For inspiration in creating your own color scheme, think of your favorite places, either in your own part of the country or farther afield. Woods and forests offer every shade of green, from mossy and pale leaf greens to intense conifer shades, and seasonal effects from the lacy cream of flowering dogwoods to the spectacular reds and golds of the fall. In prairies and meadows, soft green and gold grasses mingle with a whole spectrum of wildflowers. Mountainous landscapes provide textured grays of stone, rusty lichens, bright accents of alpine flowers, and the white of snow-capped peaks. Cultivated landscapes, too, have their own palettes. In the orchard, apples, pears, peaches, and plums are enriched with the deeper tones of raspberries, strawberries, redcurrants, and blueberries. In the vegetable garden, lettuces alone can offer a profusion of greens, along with tinges of deep red—a perfect complement to deep purple eggplants. Carrots, corn, and squash bring mellow tones of orange and gold.

This pretty cupboard is a new, inexpensive purchase from a large furniture store. For a softer look, the dark stain has been painted over with a primer, followed by eggshell.

The same pale color has been used on the walls, freestanding cupboard and closet doors. Besides being a restful shade for a bedroom, it provides a good background for the bright colors of the printed bed linens and whimsical string of lights.

thrifty looks prudent panache

Cutting back on costs doesn't mean lowering your standards. Clever, thrifty people use flair instead of money to bring class, glamour, and style to the humblest of homes. A throwaway gesture such as a scarf tied in the latest manner is all a stylish girl-about-town needs to prove she is on the fashion ball. And with a good hairdo and a wardrobe of carefully chosen basics in well-cut shapes that she knows flatter her good points and play down the not-so-good, she will always look and feel good. By adding carefully sourced extras from chain stores or thrift shops, she can create a range of looks to suit personal taste and any occasion. Employing similar techniques, it is also possible to create an interior that is classy, snazzy, swanky, or distinctly modish—not only easy on the eye but also easy on the pocket.

Perhaps you already have a house full of perfectly nice, good-quality stuff, but it lacks a certain something—a dash of panache, in fact. It may be that all that is needed is a sensational wall color or a good clean. Don't rush to throw things out or buy new; cast a critical eye over what you have, and pick out the best.

A small but perfectly put-together collection of good-quality, well-designed furnishings is a good foundation for any style. With a few prudent purchases and a dash of panache—which is free—you can create a classy splendor. Attention to detail is the key, whether it's exactly the right color, the perfect doorknob, or a witty dash of the unexpected. Making the best of what you've got—and showing it at its best—involves imaginative and unusual arrangements and clever accessorizing, together with a well-groomed, cared-for look.

Panache is often all that's required to create a convincing impression of any style. It can turn a colonial-style row house into Jane Austen Georgian by setting pretty sofas, chairs, beds, and chaise longues in sparsely furnished rooms painted in subdued beiges, grays, gray-greens, and blues, with scattered thin mats on bare floors. Eschewing modern built-in cabinets in favor of a capacious cupboard and a stone sink will keep up the pretense in the kitchen. Likewise, throw a large cloth over a nondescript table and place it center stage, ready for afternoon tea or an hour's

embroidery. And don't forget that a little self-indulgence can do you and your home some good. The perfect antidote to minimal is a little bit of French. Indulge in discreet decoration, but don't feel guilty about gilt. Do keep it under control, though. A single gilt-frame mirror is fine, but any more and you risk blowing your cover. With a little wit and wisdom and a lot of rubbing down and applications of steel wool, it is possible to transform quite vulgar reproduction, cheap French-style furniture, complete with curvaceous legs, decorative carving, and touches of gold, into convincing pastiches of the real thing. Buy pretty shapes, and paint them the colors of Jordon almonds.

Arranging furniture with panache can make small rooms seem large, large spaces feel intimate, and ordinary furniture appear special. After a good wax or a coat of paint, a small, junk-shop table can become a pretty writing desk or, with a couple of chairs and a candle, an intimate dining area.

Panache involves an approach to interiors that can enhance your lifestyle or suggest one that is more elegant, exciting, or expensive than you can strictly afford.

thrifty looks bohemian

budget buys

Indulging in a little maximalism, which can be eclectic, ethnic, romantic, or exotic, is the perfect way to achieve a big impact on a small budget. It is also a wonderful excuse to rebel against the de-cluttering police. Using throws, rugs, and wall hangings in dangerously dark, rich colors and sumptuous fabrics with an adventurous spirit, you can create an interior to suit many moods and associations—from the excitement of the souk to the peace and seductive charm of the boudoir.

Ideal for detracting from ugly surroundings and covering up shortcomings, it is also a relaxed alternative for those for whom dark and cozy is much more appealing than light and airy. Pile on the dhurries and throws, and no one need know that a truly horrible sofa or disgusting carpet lurks underneath those wonderful layers of exotic pattern and color. However, don't get too carried away, or you might end up with a rather too convincing imitation of a student bedroom or your very first studio apartment. The grown-up approach to bohemian is a little more discriminating and sophisticated, with a sense of order imposed by pruning out the grubby, tacky, or seriously shabby.

Variations on a bohemian theme include the happy, hippy look, which is essentially bare and simple but with a sprinkling of Indian bedspreads, wall hangings, pretty glass lamps, big floor cushions, and lots of candles. A spiced-up version features oriental carpets, rugs, kilims, dhurries, rich embroideries, jewel-colored walls and fabrics, plus a selection of ethnic objects including large pots, baskets, and decorative, carved wooden beds, cabinets, tables, and stools.

One source of inspiration for this look is Charleston—not the town, but an English farmhouse that was home to the painters Duncan Grant and Vanessa Bell, members of the artistic-literary Bloomsbury Group, in the early 1900s. They decorated the walls, doors, floors, fireplaces, and furniture of their house with exuberant patterns and figures. This thrifty way of turning the ordinary into the extraordinary can best be achieved by someone who possesses more than a dab of artistic talent. But even if you don't, you could use a stencil, and stick to something simple, such as a table or the doors of a small cabinet.

Another opportunity for a little opulence is the boudoir—now making a comeback as a refuge for busy women where they can re-engage with their feminine side. Indulge in silks and satins, lace and velvet, fringed shawls and pretty furnishings, including chaise longues and glamorous dressing tables, complete with stool and silver-backed hairbrushes.

indian cotton bedspreads
Plain and patterned, still to be found in ethnic shops and markets. Great for covering sofas, chairs, tables, and beds and can also be used as curtains.

african prints
Scour markets and specialist stores for lengths of fantastically colorful printed fabric, which can be used for everything from curtains to slipcovers.

cotton dhurries and kilims
Plentiful in shopping malls, markets, and warehouse stores. Some are quite small, so go for layers. Everything from bright, bold stripes to subtle traditional patterns to suit a variety of moods and styles. OK on the floor, but light colors soon look grubby. Good for covering furniture, hung at windows, or on walls.

oriental-style carpets
Pseudo-oriental carpets from markets and bargain stores are sometimes thin. If you choose the best colors, they can look convincing, especially when layered.

saris and embroidered fabrics
In some cosmopolitan cities you can find stores that stock a selection of Moroccan-style fabrics. Use for wall hangings, covers, cushions, and pure decoration. Take advantage of the colors and rich embroideries of traditional sari lengths, which make fabulous curtains or hangings around a bed.

make the most
of what you've got

In our eagerness to create a new look or way of living, it is easy to overlook the good points of what we've already got. It is also easy to believe that nothing short of a daring architectural scheme or a complete refit will bring our home up to the high standards we are now led to expect. Such schemes are expensive, and although they can be a worthwhile investment, making the most of what you've got can be a less stressful and more thrifty way of going about things.

the big picture

Unless your home is derelict or in a bad state of repair, think twice before embarking on the expense and hassle of building works, architects, and building codes, to say nothing of the stress of having building contractors in your home. There is no denying the appeal of huge spaces with acres of glass, but achieving it costs money.

You may well decide that invest is best, and major improvements will not only provide the much-needed extra space or better use of what you've already got, but also increase the value of your property. If you don't have the dough, don't despair. A lack of funds doesn't have to mean a lack of style.

Take a holistic approach to your house or apartment, and apply the practical and thrifty approach to home improvements, which makes the most of what's already there. Removing dirt, dreadful decoration, and damaged or unnecessary fixtures will reveal your home's good points, and you may be pleasantly surprised to find that a relatively inexpensive program of repairs, rearranging the space, and a cheering coat of paint will produce the home you've always wanted and didn't know you had.

open up

Knocking down walls may give you the loft look, but it can cost a lot both in terms of work and, if you are not careful, a reduction in the value of your property. Some people are putting walls back, and as the pleasures of large space and open-plan living become outweighed by the lack of privacy and the extra noise of family life

You may, however, still hanker for the light and airy look, and there are less drastic, and less expensive, ways of achieving it. Just removing the doors between the kitchen, hall, and living areas will make a difference. If this is likely to bring about an unacceptable level of noise or a problem with cooking smells, then think carefully, but even propping doors open semi-permanently will create an impression of more space. If you open up other areas to permanent view, you will maximize the illusion of one big space, particularly if you continue the same decorative scheme throughout all the rooms. One of the most effective ways of doing this is by restricting yourself to one floor finish and one wall color and using this throughout the space, so that the rooms appear to flow into one another.

knock through

While the thrifty approach may preclude major building works, knocking down one wall is relatively easy and not very expensive. Most people opt to increase the size of a kitchen or living area by knocking through into adjacent rooms, sometimes opening up the space completely to create a "great room" for cooking, dining, and sitting.

Alternatively, you could also consider knocking through into a hallway—a space that is often underused and may have windows that will bring in extra light. It does, however, mean being open to the stairs (if any) and bedrooms, so again before making a decision, consider whether there may be any noise or smell pollution problems. This works particularly well if you have an enclosed entryway; if not, then make provision for draft-proofing the front door during the colder months.

glaze over

The main attraction of large spaces is that they are, or appear to be, full of light. A cheaper alternative to removing walls is to replace solid doors with glass ones, which come in a variety of styles and with different kinds of glass.

Replacing a window with glass-paneled French doors is not too much

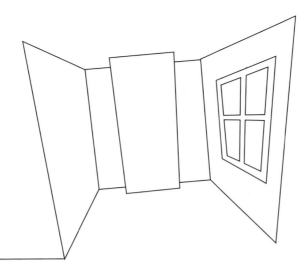

trouble and will make a room not only lighter but more elegant. For a dramatic effect, replace a whole wall with large patio doors. This will be more expensive, as it entails putting in supporting beams and employing experts, but even so, it's not hugely expensive for the impact that it will give.

By adding a sunroom to your house, you can enjoy plenty of natural light, even in winter. A cheaper odption is a lean-to greenhouse; there's no law saying you have to use it exclusively for plants.

rethink your space

If moving or getting in an architect are simply not viable options, it is possible to achieve amazing results by just changing how you allocate and utilize your space. Consider turning your house upside down by moving living areas upstairs and bedrooms downstairs. This will make the most of the upstairs space, views, and sunshine during the daytime. If you crave privacy, a small, seldom-used storage room could double as a private retreat, and a generous bedroom could provide a sitting area that is out of bounds to the rest of the household. Make the most of

any nooks and crannies, especially the space under the stairs, which is usually given over to storage but could successfully be made into a powder room or shower room, opened up and fitted out as a work area, or used as extra seating-cum-spare bed.

We all know that rooms with less clutter look bigger. Although a wall of purpose-built cabinets may take up a reasonable slice of your room, they will accommodate huge amounts of stuff and equipment. In a kitchen, large cabinets can house almost everything, including a washing machine and a dishwasher. The benefits of proper storage for clothes are obvious; likewise, a heap of toys or even a whole office can be hidden away in the evenings to free up the room for more restful or recreational activities.

Attic conversions can be a lot cheaper than moving, as well as adding value to your present home, but it is certainly not a cheap option and needs to be done by a professional who will make sure that work is carried out properly and complies with your local building codes. Don't forget to consult

your neighbors; you may need permission from them to carry out any work on party walls. Before you get too excited, make sure there is room for a proper staircase—a pull-down or rope version is OK for infrequent visits, but is no good for regular use. For rooms with sloping ceilings, a dormer window can increase the usable space; but beware the building codes, and think carefully how it will look from the outside. A badly designed scheme not only will look horrible; it could seriously affect the value of your home.

If you've really run out of room indoors but have spare space outdoors, get a shed. A small shed can take the pressure off indoor storage, and even a modest-sized version can act as summer house, playhouse, studio, office, or refuge.

a coat of paint

Paint is eminently affordable, making it possible to perform miracles of transformation for a surprisingly small sum.

walls and woodwork

A coat of paint provides you with the proverbial "blank canvas" upon which to create your own picture of domestic life. Any house can be made brighter and better if it is painted throughout in white or a pale neutral color, with the added advantage that it will look and feel bigger—particularly good for small houses or rooms.

If you have a plain or relatively characterless house, you will find that its shortcomings are less obvious with careful use of paint—unattractive features can be painted into the background by using the same color for walls and paintwork. Paint over rough, damaged, or patchy surfaces, and you will find that imperfections become virtually invisible, especially when your possessions are in place.

For characterful and architecturally beautiful homes, a coat of paint emphasizes good points and pleasing proportions and allows distinguishing features to stand out. Pick out quality woodwork in super glossy or muted matte paint in harmonizing or contrasting colors.

floors

Bare floors are all the rage. If you have floorboards that are in good condition, it is relatively easy and inexpensive to strip them and turn them into a fashionable feature. If the boards are a bit rough, give them a good coating of floor paint, which is hard-wearing and now available in many of the trendy colors.

Better-quality boards can take the more subtle watercolor approach, using washes of latex flat sealed with a robust matte varnish or waxed and allowed to acquire the well-worn look. Use light colors, especially if the room is small or dark. Dark or bright colors can look great but could become oppressive and drive you mad after a while. Do a good job—prepare well and paint carefully.

furniture

A coat of paint covers up dull, dirty, or damaged wood and old paint. It's a well-known fact that painting a jumble of mismatched chairs the same color will create a quirky but matching set. Equally, a set of ordinary chairs can be enlivened by painting them different colors. Whether they are old or new, prosaic or characterful, tables, cabinets, chests of drawers, storage chests and trunks, bookcases, and shelves can all be transformed and rehabilitated with a coat of paint. A thick coating of white gloss paint disciplines even the scruffiest piece of furniture, while dull matte can add sophistication. Convert starkly new into convincingly old, using simple but attractive paint effects.

built-in furniture

Built-in cabinets and shelves are useful but not always very attractive or interesting. You can, however, minimize or maximize their impact with a coat of paint. Use the same color as the walls if you want them to blend into the background, but for a bit of fun, turn them into a feature with color.

In this small house, the use of a single color on the walls, furniture, and fixtures unifies the space, making it seem much larger and maximizing the light.

Any room can look bright, clean, and beautiful after a liberal application of white or very pale paint. Hard-wearing gloss paint accentuates the good points of a piece of furniture or woodwork, and protecting the surface, it can easily be wiped clean.

style check fashion update

Before consigning your possessions to the charity collection or garage sale, take another look. It's easy to take things for granted and to hang on to old prejudices regarding style. Fashions change, and designs that were once consigned to the back of the closet may now be the height of chic, so take a second look, and you may find a treasure trove of things you didn't know you liked.

fancy china

Tea sets and dinner services evoke a more formal and leisurely approach to dining. For thrifty people, for whom eating in is the new eating out, taking tea and dining formally are not only a great antidote to fast food and fast living but an opportunity to appreciate good food. Brighten up new plain dishes by mixing in a few pretty florals.

lamps

Modern lighting design is sleek and functional, and much of it is very inexpensive. But don't dismiss old lamp bases or floor lamps, as they can be given a new lease on life with a plain drum shade, and some even look OK with just a bare bulb, especially as there are lots of new shapes to choose from. However, old-fashioned shades look quirky and friendly, so why not hang on to them?

dining table and chairs

Dining tables and matching chairs are sometimes
rejected as old-fashioned, but give them a second
chance. A good-sized table and set of chairs in a
kitchen or living room may inspire "proper" family
mealtimes, and one of the best way of entertaining
friends is around a table full of good food and
wine. The dining-room table also provides space
for homework, sewing, and other homely pursuits.

sideboards

Sideboards are back in favor, for they are incredibly
useful. Traditionally a home for table linens, drinks,
and glasses, they still perform that function very
well but are also good for CDs, DVDs, and even
sound systems. Learn to appreciate the solid
wood versions from the 1930s and '40s, the
lighter, more idiosyncratic shapes from the 1950s,
and the long, low ones from the 1960s and '70s.

Hide an ugly frame and make reading in bed more comfortable with a quilt draped over the headboard. Old ones look special, but there are plenty of pretty new ones at reasonable prices.

Beside rejuvenating the bed frame, cover worn springs with wooden slats, and replace a saggy old mattress with a new one. Complete the rehabilitation by investing in new pillows and duvets, and bed linen from widely available, ever-expanding, good-quality, but modestly priced ranges.

reuse and recycle

Instead of throwing furniture out because it is unattractive, or perhaps doesn't quite perform the right function, use a little creative imagination to see whether you can use it in a different context or guise. A bit of re-invention can turn an item into a useful, smart, and even special piece of furniture.

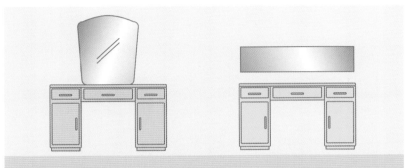

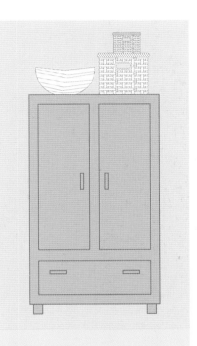

dressing table

The humble dressing table, deemed old-fashioned and outmoded, was discarded in favor of more closet space. But recently it has been sneaking back into fashion, along with the penchant for glamour and dressing up. Reconfigure and rejuvenate it with a coat of paint in a brilliant, unexpected color. If necessary, remove any damaged or really ugly mirrors, moldings, knobs, and handles, and replace them with new or funky alternatives.

chest of drawers and dressers

If you've got your clothes storage sorted out and find you have a spare chest of drawers, it could be given a new lease on life in the kitchen. The drawers of a chest can be used for anything from table linen to packages of rice. Hang an inexpensive shelf unit above it, paint them both the same color and you have an instant kitchen dresser—a place to store and show off your best china.

armoire

Don't hide your hallway under a pile of coats, bags, and shoes. Store everything in that armoire you were about to throw out. If there are shelves for scarves, hats, and other accessories, so much the better. Alternatively, hang one of those canvas pockets inside for just such a purpose. Use the space on top for storage, perhaps with a colorful basket for seasonal accessories.

good housekeeping clean it up

When a home is looking tired and scruffy, it's too easy to think that nothing short of a complete makeover will bring it back to life. We often take our surroundings for granted, seeing only the dull finishes, stains, worn edges, and general lackluster appearance, rather than appreciating the good properties and personalities of our homes. We all know how a room responds to a quick tidy and a bit of fresh air, so think what a thorough wash and brush-up could do.

Cleaning has been described as the new sex. This may be stretching a point, but there is no doubt that good housekeeping has gained a higher profile in recent years. Some of the most popular visitor events at big English country houses are the "below stairs" activities, including spring cleaning and the care of textiles, furniture, and precious objects. Instead of a makeover that will cost money and involve decisions about new schemes, why not give your space a healthy dose of TLC? This is not only the cheaper option but a thrifty one, too, as it will ensure that your furniture and furnishings last longer.

a good clean

Start at the top of your house, or apartment, so that you are not passing through already cleaned areas to get to the unclean. Take down any draperies or curtains, and remove slipcovers from sofas, chairs, and cushions. Take down blinds and any other window coverings, so that you can give the window a thorough clean.

Launder any washable fabrics, using a gentle detergent. It is not necessary to dry-clean heavy draperies or slipcovers every year, so if they have been cleaned in the recent past, just give them a good vacuum, using the narrow nozzle to get down the sides and backs of chairs and sofas. Treat any marks with a stain remover.

Wash, dry-clean or vacuum Roman shades. Plastic or metal blinds can be washed in the bathtub or under the shower using mild detergent or spray cleaners. Wooden blinds should be dusted or wiped with a damp cloth (do this before taking them down, as it is easier to do this in situ).

Using a vacuum cleaner, get rid of the dust from all surfaces, including floors, walls, ceilings, and doors. Make sure you get into all corners and moldings. Use the small nozzle of the vacuum cleaner along the edges between the baseboard and the floor.

It's not necessary to wash walls (it is easier and more fun to repaint them), but obvious dirt and stains around light switches or areas of heavy traffic can be removed with mild detergent. However, you might end up with an obvious clean patch, so it may be best to wash the whole wall or repaint. Instead of fully repainting, it is possible to freshen up latex paint with watered-down paint (approximately one part paint to two parts water). Apply with a paintbrush rather than a roller.

Wash all woodwork, using a soft scouring sponge for excess goo, but don't scrub too hard, as you will destroy the surface and encourage more dirt. Dry with soft cotton cloths (dish towels are good).

Vacuum carpets thoroughly, and shampoo if really necessary. Try not to do this too often, as it destroys some of the stain retardants and natural properties of the fibers, so that carpets then get dirty more quickly. Waxed or oiled wooden floors should be repolished or oiled. Wash varnished floors with a damp mop or cloth, and apply another coat of varnish if the surface shows bad signs of wear. Painted floors can be mopped using mild detergent and should be repainted or resealed if in a bad state. Use soap rather than detergent to wash stone floors. Ceramic tiles and vinyl will always benefit from a good scrub.

spring clean sense

Protect yourself from splashes, bashes, and harmful chemicals by wearing gloves, a smock, and sensible shoes with the laces carefully fastened. Don't wear baggy trousers, as you could trip over them. Always tie back long hair or wrap it up in a scarf.

Begin at the top of the house or the equivalent in an appartment, so that you are not passing through cleaned areas to get to the unclean. Start at the top—ceilings first, floors last.

Protect and preserve – cover furniture and floors with a drop cloth or plastic sheeting and protect vulnerable corners with old blankets.

First get rid of any dust from all surfaces (a vacuum cleaner is good for this). Dust turns to dirt when it comes into contact with water, so removing it reduces cleaning, particularly on surfaces that are to be washed down.

If cleaning really isn't your thing, consider getting in a professional company to do the job. Obviously, it will cost more, but it can be the thrifty option, especially if you have valuable furniture and furnishings or a high-quality flooring, such as parquet or stone, which needs careful treatment.

10 tools for janitor joy

drop cloths

Cover furniture to keep out dust and any splashes that could damage or stain surfaces and fabrics. A good way to put old sheets to use; but for precious items, add extra protection in the form of plastic sheeting.

good-quality cotton cloths

Old cotton sheets make good cloths, as cotton is better at serious cleaning than disposable wipes. Squeeze out for a non-smear finish, wash, and reuse. Cotton dust cloths don't leave fluff behind and can be laundered.

specialist products

Although often expensive, specialist cleaners can give good results. Before buying, read the label to check that it is the right product for the job—using the wrong cleaner can seriously damage materials and surfaces.

feather dusters

Gentle but efficient. Particularly good for cleaning books and precious items that get very dusty. Long-handled versions deal with fine cobwebs, but long-handled brushes may be better for the larger, spookier variety.

sponges and scourers

Good for stubborn stains and dirty deposits. Use gentler, non-stick pan sponges for delicate surfaces. Nylon scourers are great dirtbusters for all jobs, from preparing paintwork to scrubbing down wooden furniture.

ecocleaning

Distilled white vinegar is the new star of the cleaning department. It is highly effective in removing grease and lime and soap deposits. Mixed with baking soda, white vinegar makes an effective surface cleaner.

mops, brooms, and brushes

Soft brooms get fine dust and debris out from corners and along baseboards. A dustpan and brush are essential companions to the broom, but a short-handled brush is useful for awkward corners and stairs.

vacuum cleaner

The only efficacious way to get dust out of carpets, draperies, upholstery, and beds. Good for bare floors, too. Buy one with a good set of tools for cleaning corners and crannies. Don't forget to empty the bag frequently!

stepladder

Don't risk life and limb balancing on makeshift or rickety ladders. Lightweight aluminum stepladders are inexpensive and easy to move around and provide a safe way of reaching ceilings, tops of walls, and windows.

mild detergent and bleach

Mild detergent is sufficient for general cleaning, including windows. Gentle household soap suits delicate surfaces, while bleach is an efficient germ killer, with whitening and stain-removing powers. Dilute and use sparingly.

instant freshen-ups

fresh air and ventilation

Just one exhaled breath on a windowpane or mirror creates mist and smears, Multiply that by the thousands of breaths you take every day, then add in the steam from baths, showers, cooking, dish washing, and laundry, and you begin to understand the importance of good ventilation. Consider also the number of germs set free in day-to-day life, plus the chemicals and pollutants released by cleaning materials, cosmetics, and beauty products, then add in the chemicals present in carpets, fabrics, paints, and building materials, and chances are it won't be long before you get the urge to open a window.

We are, however, encouraged to conserve the expensive and potentially planet-harming energy we all use in heating our homes by insulating, sealing up holes, and making sure windows and doors are draft-free. Add to this our (often necessary) obsession with security, and you end up living in a hermetically sealed environment with poor air circulation, which affects our health and that of our home and its contents. The results of poor ventilation include condensation, mold, mildew, stuffiness, and unpleasant smells.

smelling sweet

A fresh-smelling, well-ventilated home will make you feel healthier and more alert, but avoid using artificial deodorizers or room scents, as many of them contain a cocktail of chemicals that mask smells by manipulating your olfactory senses. Keep things natural, and stick to scented plants, flowers, candles, and oils.

A few drops of essential oil in water heated over a flame in a ceramic oil-burner will scent the air and set a mood. Investigate the properties of various oils. Lavender is known for its relaxing properties, whereas rosemary is a good pep-you-up. A specialist can create a formula to suit your personality and requirements. Use scented candles only if you can afford the good ones with natural ingredients; don't even think about buying the cheap ones, as their smells will almost certainly be chemically based and will pollute rather than clear the air.

A vase of flowers cheers up the grimmest room, and if they are scented, all the better. Go for subtle rather than pungent perfumes, and opt for seasonal blooms to harmonize with body rhythms and enhance well-being. Roses smell best in summer, narcissi enhance the

freshness of spring, and winter jasmine raises the spirits. If you have a garden or even a window box, select plants for their scent, which, wafted in through an open window, is the best room freshener of all.

thrifty consumer

Conspicuous consumption is so last year. Nonetheless, thrifty people with shopaholic tendencies don't have to miss out on their favorite pastime. In fact, a nose for a bargain, an instinct for what is likely to be the next big thing, plus a willingness to spend hours in pursuit of the perfect purchase are great assets, as long as they are accompanied by self-control, a clear idea of what you are looking for, an ability to say no, and the patience to wait for what you really want.

buying old where to shop

Antiques are expectedly pricey. "Second-hand" used to mean cheap until "retro" became big business; competition and prices are escalating. The plethora of TV programs inflating the value of anything old, from a cabinet to a cookie tin, has also raised the stakes, so sellers are less likely to let things go for a song. Getting real bargains is becoming more difficult, but a keen eye and an ability to see beyond any shortcomings can still bring rewards, as well as being good fun.

antique and vintage dealers

There is a perception that genuine antiques are very expensive, but prices often compare favorably with the high end of new and the rising cost of "retro." While rare antiques or examples of fine craftsmanship will be costly, the plainer, more solid stuff is often good value. Cultivate a friendship with local antique dealers to pick up useful tips. If you have a preference for particular styles and eras, they will keep an eye open for fine examples at good prices for you. The genuine article usually costs money, but sometimes it is worth it, as you cannot rely on happenstance to pick up what you are looking for. Use these dealers to learn what to look out for so you will recognize a lucky bargain in thrift shops and rummage and garage sales.

antique fairs and markets

The important antique fairs are held in exhibition centers, hotels, and town halls; appeal to serious collectors; and often involve serious money. The vendors are professionals, so don't expect very low prices. More modest affairs, held in streets, marketplaces, and community centers, are more modestly priced. But in any market, prices can vary from genuine bargains to scandalously overpriced, so knowledge is a fine thing. Research the market to get some idea of what to look for and what is a fair price.

salesrooms

Look before you buy, examine the piece, and make sure it is what you want. Prices vary, depending on how trendy the item is and how many dealers are bidding. Remember, a dealer needs to sell his or her goods on at a much higher price, but a winning bid could still be below the market value. Visit a few sales before deciding to make a bid; then you'll get some idea of prices and what type of stuff is still cheap. Consider all of an item's good points, and decide whether it is suitable for you or could be the next fashion. If you are willing to pay a good price for something you really want, make sure it is in good condition. Paying top dollar for something you have to spend a lot of time and money on putting right is not thrift sense.

flea markets

The distinction between antique and flea markets is blurred, but flea markets are usually held outdoors. Small town markets in less touristy or trendy areas are more likely to yield bargains. Markets in different countries offer a less familiar, and possibly more interesting, selection of goods.

salvage yards

Great places for finding old doors, window frames, floorboards, moldings, stone sinks, clawfoot bathtubs, and many unusual items of architectural interest. It can be expensive, as this sort of stuff is in great demand, but may be worth the expense if you want to replace original

fixtures in properties where sensitive restoration is a worthwhile investment.

used office equipment suppliers

Besides desks, chairs, and filing cabinets, you can also find tables and upholstered seating. Among the steel tubing and laminate (a good "modern" material), you may find solid wood or metal desks, wooden flat files, and sometimes old filing systems and pigeon-holes that make great storage. School chairs, lockers, and cabinets offer good-quality design at reasonable prices.

internet shopping

Trading on the Internet is increasing in popularity. It's not the same as poking around in dusty curiosity shops, but if you're after something special, you can search the whole world via the mouse. It's also a useful reference for checking the value of what you want to buy or sell. Use only reputable sites, and exercise caution when paying for anything over the Net. For private sales or purchases from smaller stores, make contact by telephone, and ensure you have all the seller's details before making a payment.

secondhand and junk shops

Poking around in a crowded junk shop full of potential gems and bargains is, for many people, one of life's great pleasures. Frequent visits are recommended to get the pick of any new stock. Look for the smaller items from house clearances, such as sets of table linen and china. Prices vary, but they are the sort of places where you can make an offer. Consignment shops—secondhand shops that sell items for individuals, with the shopkeeper taking a percentage of the price—can be useful if you want to dispose of old furnishings. The price you receive can then be applied to purchasing new ones.

thrift shops

Run by charities, thrift shops have traditionally been great places to pick up bargains of all kinds, and some specialize in furniture and household accessories. However, some thrift shops have gone upscale, with prices to match. If you're decorating on a shoestring, focus on those less-affluent neighborhoods.

garage and yard sales

Trawling through sales by individual households is a fairly hit-and-miss way of finding bargains, but you might be lucky Make sure to get there early.

rummage sales

You stand a better chance of bagging a bargain at a rummage sale, because the stuff isn't sorted beforehand: the volunteers in charge are not always tuned in to the latest design trends. The best buys are in affluent areas, where the castoffs are likely to be of good quality.

classified ads

Fun to read, and you never know what might turn up.

dumpsters

There are still exciting things lurking in dumpsters, but you have get in there first. You have to be brazen enough to pillage in broad daylight in full view of passersby. Duncan Phyfe chairs are rare finds, but furniture from the 1960s and '70s is not. Perfectly good rugs are often chucked out, and it's worth looking in plastic bags, for curtains and other textiles. Office furniture is often found in dumpsters.

10 still-affordable things

hall stands

They add character to any hallway, as well as keeping coats, hats, and umbrellas under control. Occasionally they are found in solid oak, but most often in dark wood, which could look better painted. Some have a mirror.

rugs and mats

They can often be bought at giveaway prices. If they're a bit grubby, they may respond well to carpet shampoo. Threadbare is chic. Use several rugs in layers, with the not-so-attractive ones at the bottom.

bed frames

Proper bed frames, especially wooden ones, are back in fashion. If the supporting base is missing, it is not too difficult to make a new slatted one from inexpensive lumber.

armchairs with wooden arms

There is a plentiful supply of smart armchairs, which are neither as big nor as expensive as a fully upholstered chair so are good for small spaces. They can also be freshened up easily and cheaply with a tie-on chair cover.

small cabinets

Whether they are delightfully dilapidated or freshened up with a new coat of paint, you're bound to find a use for a pretty little cabinet or shelf. Hang wall cabinets in twos and threes—they don't have to match.

doorknobs and handles

It's not essential to have matching doorknobs throughout your house, or even matching knobs on a single piece of furniture. If you find something special, put it to good use.

lamp bases

Lamps are simple to update with a fashionable new shade, but they can also look good with just a bulb. Watch for tall floor lamps.

wallpaper

Wallcoverings are back—and the older the better. Wallpaper you would have taken the stripper to only a few years ago suddenly looks great.

odd tiles

If you like the casual look and are feeling creative, a patchwork of tiles in a kitchen or bathroom can strike exactly the right note.

kitchen equipment

Keep an eye out for old storage tins, utensils, pots, pans, bread bins, cake tins, breadboards, and cutlery.

buying old what to look for

armoires and dressing tables

With more people than ever tuned in to the changing trends in interiors and the retro and vintage market, it is becoming harder to find real bargains. It is still possible, however, to pick up old armoires and dressing tables made from thin, not very nice wood with an unpleasant shiny varnished finish. These are still quite cheap, so snap them up, put on a coat of primer to ensure that the paint will stick, and give them a color makeover using unexpected and brilliant shades. Reconfigure them by removing any damaged or really ugly mirrors, moldings, knobs, and handles, and give them funky new replacements.

desks

Incredibly useful for keeping all the invoices, bills, birth certificates, passports, and other paperwork that we all accumulate. A pull-down top provides space for a laptop computer or for writing good old-fashioned letters. Look beyond first impressions; if the finish is not very appealing, give it a coat of paint or stain.

utilitarian furniture

A lot of basic, solid furniture made in the 1930s and '40s is often overlooked because of its lack of distinguishing style details, but the quality of the materials and workmanship is high, and the simple designs allow them to fit into most interiors. Made mostly from solid wood, it needs only a good clean and repolish or a coat of paint. Look for similar office, school, and hospital furniture from the same period.

turn of the century

Fashionable in the 1960s for those setting up home on a shoestring, the curvy, decorative, and often large-scale furniture of the early 1900s was very popular. However, the fashion for minimal interiors has lessened its appeal, so it should be possible to find a few bargains in the form of dining tables and chairs, large chiffoniers, armchairs, and sofas. Look for small delicate tables, cake stands, trays, odd bits of china, cutlery, cruet sets, and pieces of silver.

picture frames and mirrors

There are still bargains to be had. Look especially for large, fancy picture frames, and smarten them up or tone them down with paint. Seek out old, shaped mirrors usually hung by a chain, traditionally placed above a mantelpiece but equally at home in a bedroom or bathroom. They look fun when hung in twos and threes.

linens

Old cotton and linen is often thicker and softer than their new equivalents, and prices can still be surprisingly low. Besides sheets and pillowcases, look for tablecloths, runners, napkins, and antimacassars, especially if they are hand-embroidered or edged in lace.

blankets, rugs, and throws

With duvets becoming increasingly popular, there are plenty of blankets lurking in secondhand stores, rummage sales, and thrift shops. Pick out any clean, good-quality woolen blankets, and give them a good wash. You may be lucky and find old ones with fashionable stripes or windowpane checks, but the traditional cream or even pink blankets can look very good and cozy. Also, don't forget to take a second look at those candlewick bedspreads.

buying old best invest

Along with "vintage," the term "antique" is now used to describe any desirable and fashionable style from rococo to retro. Encouraged by TV programs that reveal the potentially high value of our possessions, far more people are now in the know. This makes for a much more competitive market, with higher prices, which is bad news for low budgets. However, sometimes it's sound thrift sense to invest in good-quality pieces that will last for many years and appreciate in value. Here is a brief roundup of currently popular styles.

colonial period

Probably the most prized of all antiques are the elegant pieces of furniture produced in the late 17th and 18th centuries, in such styles as baroque, Queen Anne, and Geogian. Some of these were imported from Britain; others were made by skilled colonial craftsmen. Needless to say, such pieces are very scarce, and this is reflected in their steep prices and in the proliferation of fakes created to meet the demand. Simple country furniture of this period, though considerably less expensive, is also much sought-after. If you have money to invest in an authentic example of colonial furniture, have it examined by an expert first.

shaker

The religious sect known as the Shakers first settled in American Colonies in the 1770s. They produced a uniquely American style of furniture—elegantly simple and ingenious in its design and made with superb craftsmanship. Partly because it harmonizes so well with modern interiors, it has recently become enormously fashionable—and expensive.

Victorian period

The long reign of Queen Victoria (1837–1901) spanned a profusion of furnishing styles, most of them revivals of earllier styles, such as medieval and Renaissance. Most of these—the ones generaly dubbed "Victorian"—are characterized by highly elaborate carving, overstuffed upholstery, and sheer bulk. This heavy look has long been out of favor; and for this reason, and because much more furniture was produced in this period than in Colonial times, bargains are relatively plentiful. You might not want to furnish your home in Victorian style, but one or more pieces, such as a mirror, some dining chairs, or an armoire, could add a note of distinction to an otherwise plain interior.

A reaction against the florid Victorian style and its often inferior workmanship began in the late 1800s. This was the Arts and Crafts movement, spearheaded by the English designer William Morris. Arts and Crafts furniture ranges from solid-looking cabinets, settles, and dressers to more delicate, rush-seated chairs, all carefully crafted by hand. An American variant of Arts and Crafts, called the Mission style, flourished in the early 1900s and has recently become fashionable again.

twentieth-century modern

This term is used to describe a wide range of modernist furniture, from the design classics of the Bauhaus era to the more recent designs of the 1960s and '70s. Much of the furniture from these later periods has only just been rediscovered; things that were destined for skips a few years ago are now fetching eyebrow-raising prices. Knowing your styles and designers is essential, so consult some of the excellent books on the subject. If you can't afford a piece of furniture, console yourself with accessories, such as glasswear, ceramics, or textiles. Or consider Retro style, a subcategory of Modern. The term usually applies to anything reminiscent of the 1940s and '50s diner look, with lots of chrome, leather, plastics, and bright colors. A few pieces of Retro could give an uninspiring room a bit of pizzazz.

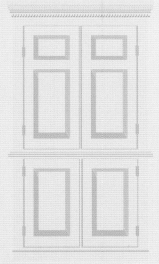

late 18th-century armoire

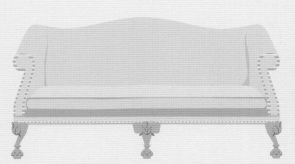

late 18th-century scroll-armed sofa

arts and crafts dresser

art deco upholstered armchair

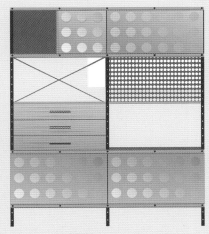

1950s modular storage system

1950s lounge chair

1950s upholstered armchair

1960s pendant lamp

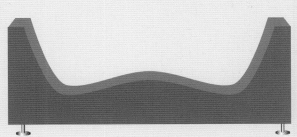

1960s seating system

buying old a word of caution

appliances

Modern appliances are safe and efficient, but with a few (mostly expensive) alternatives, their design tends to be hard-edged. For the most part they are available only in clinical white or stainless steel, which can spoil the effect of a retro-style or lived-in-look kitchen. For this reason, old refrigerators and ranges are very popular, and although some are fetching premium prices in specialist stores and on Web sites, it's possible to pick up something for a lower price than for a modern equivalent.

lighting

There are still lots of bargains to be had. Look for desk lamps, lamp bases, and shades from the 1930s and '40s. Central hanging fixtures, often featuring colored or patterned glass, were popular from the 1950s to '70s; once much reviled, they are now de rigueur. Chandeliers are also back in favor, and odd pretty glass lamp shades can still be quite cheap. Check all plugs, cables, and cords, and replace with new if they look at all questionable. You can buy old-fashioned twisted cord for authenticity.

electrical goods

Your best guide to the safety of an electrical appliance, new or used, id the UL (Underwriters' Laboratory) sign of approval on it. In the case of a secondhand appliance, it's best also to have it checked first by an electrician. As with lighting, check all cables and connections. Don't forget that foreign appliances are likely to be incompatible with the electricity supply.

gas ranges

You can find good bargains among the secondhand gas ranges offered by local dealers or over the Internet. Some retailers may also have outdated floor models for sale at good prices. But you should be aware that installing any gas appliance requires a permit in accordance with your local codes. Have the range installed by a licensed gas fitter, who should obtain the permit for you.

radiators

Bulky cast-iron radiators are now considered very stylish, so if you have this kind of heating, you might like to stick with it, rather than upgrading to a more modern system. If you want to buy this kind of radiator, you can often find them in salvage yards; however, they're often not very efficient, so get an expert to give them the once-over.

woodworm

Check any wooden items for signs of live woodworm: fresh holes and deposits of sawdust are a reliable indication. For small items, it is relatively easy to treat the infestation using a proprietary product that can be either brushed on or squirted into the holes using a syringe. It may be wise to treat any troublesome item before bringing it into your home; that way, you won't allow the pests the run of the rest of your house.

buying new what to look for

There was a time when good design and fashionable style were available only at the high, and expensive, end of the market. Today you can find both in a wide variety of places, from the big out-of-town warehouses to shopping-mall chains and bargain stores. Now that we are offered a huge selection of simple, good-looking furniture and fixtures at remarkably low prices, "cheap" has ceased to be a derogatory term. In fact, many low-cost items have become modern classics and can be found in the most gracious, as well as the most humble, homes.

Thrift isn't only about low prices; it also takes into account issues of value, suitability, and sustainability. Buying for the short term may solve current budget deficiencies, but may turn out to have been a false economy if the goods need replacing soon after.

price control

When you buy something at the top end of the market, you pay more for style, quality, and exclusivity. If you pay less, you may have to compromise on one or more of these.

It is now acknowledged that too much consumer choice causes stress and anxiety; faced with the profusion of products available for the home, it's easy to see why. Weighing up your options and balancing your budget can turn shopping into a far from relaxing activity, especially when the price of an item isn't always related to its quality or value.

Some stores specialize in a certain type of product and are therefore able to sell it more cheaply, while larger retailers with greater spending power and bulk orders can also afford to keep prices low. It is possible, therefore, to find price variations within ranges of similar items.

Doing your homework, shopping around, and examining the product in question will help identify the best value. A flexible attitude to budgets is also helpful. While thrifty people want, or need, to avoid high prices, it is always worth looking at the more expensive option, as the difference in quality or style may be worth much more than the difference in price. For a fairly modest upgrade, you may get a far better buy.

basic instincts

Since everyone buys clothes from large chain stores, wise shoppers know not to buy distinctive designs, in order to avoid advertising exactly where you shop and meeting other people similarly dressed. Smart shoppers buy the basics and then accessorize them so as to create a style that is their own. This applies equally to interiors; canny customers buy items that will be a discreet presence rather than a bold statement. Some department stores may appear dated and dull, but look carefully at the merchandise, as you may find a simple, inoffensive design that is of much higher quality, and better priced, than its equivalent in a more trendy store.

long-lasting

As already stated, we live in a throw-away age, buying cheap items designed to last only a short time before being disposed of and replaced with new. Unfortunately, we are running out of room to dispose of all the rubbish, added to which it is a tremendous waste of precious resources and a threat to the environment. Buying less but spending more in the first place not only will help save the planet but will help you save money in the long run. For example, it may seem to make sense to buy an inexpensive sofa if it is going to be subjected to the ravages of children or pets, but a more expensive, better-quality item will be able to withstand such use and can be cleaned or re-covered over time.

lasting impression

Fashions come and go, but classics stay the course. Spend money on quality and good, but simple designs that are capable of living through the fads and fancies of one era and obligingly fit in with the next. Remember also that it is often better to blow the budget on one or two good pieces, as they will be the center of attraction for now and the core of a collection for the future.

salesmanship

If you have champagne tastes but a soda pop budget, the sales are for you. Keep an eye on the smartest stores, and make sure you know when their sales are on. Join their mailing list or check Web sites regularly for special offers, reductions, stock clearances, or even closing-down sales. Most high-class stores have sale previews, so go along to see if it's worth packing the thermos and sandwiches for a long wait in line and a chance of getting your chosen bargain. Besides great sale reductions, stores often run a 10% or more discount offer on normal stock, which can make the previously unaffordable just about possible. Visit sales in their late stages, when prices are further reduced. With managers anxious to get rid of stuff, the bargains are better, and stores may be open to offers.

quality control

The difficulty now is not finding something cheap but knowing what to choose. Here are a few guidelines.

solid wood

Some of the cheapest furniture available is made from fiberboard, laminated with wood or plastic. Although it may look OK, the edges are prone to damage. Solid wood looks and wears better and can be treated with paint, stain, or wax to improve its life expectancy.

dimensions

The success of a well-designed piece of furniture rests on its proportions and dimensions, as well as on the materials and styling. Cost cutting can sometimes lead to a less generous use of materials, which in the poorest examples results in a mean and cheap-looking product. Opt for designs that look robust—chunky rather than thin.

color and finish

Inexpensive fabrics and laminates can look cheap in bright colors, so stick to whites and neutrals. Soft woods are sometimes given a coating of durable varnish to make them more hard-wearing, but it can look horrible. Paint or stain can cover such inadequacies.

safety in numbers

A cheap item on its own draws attention to itself, but gains confidence in a group. Inexpensive bookcases are remarkable value and look convincing when several are placed together.

best invest

The best modern design is elegant, seductive, perfectly formed, beautifully made, and usually very expensive. If Modernism is your passion and only the best will do, the thrifty solution is to forego vacations, evenings out, and a fully furnished house in order to purchase something special. A single item, such as a superb chair by Alvar Aalto, Hans Wegner, or Ico Parisi, or a piece of decorative glass by Tapio Wirkkala, is enough to add class and charisma to a whole interior. Just remember to keep the competition at bay and showcase your star attraction in a simple, pared-down setting.

Original modern designs can increase in value, so as long as you look after them, they may be a good investment. If you are clever and can spot an up-and-coming designer, scour art school exhibitions for collectibles of the future. You could even commission a piece made to your specifications.

Truly good design never dates; in fact, it gets better with age. Investing in genuine design classics is always a good idea, but if you don't have the resources, there are plenty of good imitations around with the same clean lines and shapes. Mass production has led to a high level of quality at surprisingly low prices.

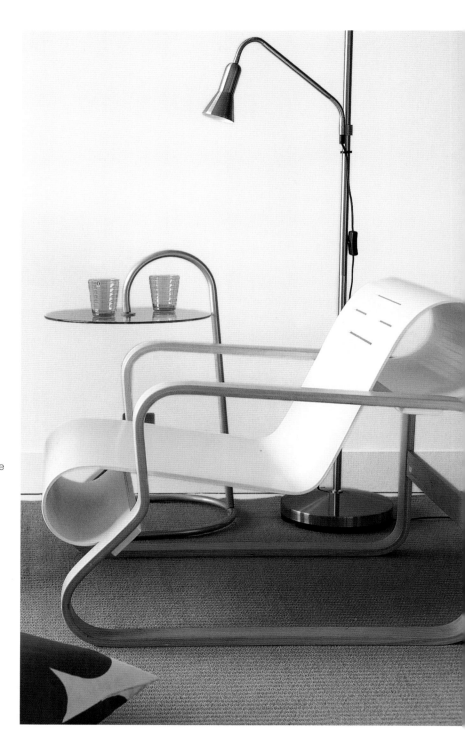

buying new cheapo classics

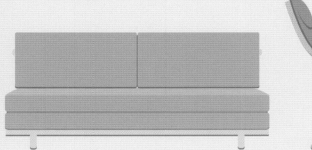

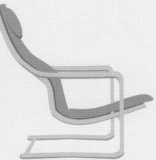

studio couch

Made up of square-edged cushions on a metal frame, this type of sofa is usually inexpensive. It looks smarter, and takes up less space, than a futon. It looks good left plain or softened with pillows and throws.

plywood frame armchair

Reminiscent of the designs of Marcel Breuer and Bruno Matthson; but the fact that it is not a direct copy makes this chair a classic in its own right. Very comfortable, especially with a matching footstool.

plywood dining chair

The popularity and versatility of Arne Jacobsen's Series 7 chairs have led to a number of imitations. Some are more blatant than others, but all possess an elegance and give the opportunity for a splash of color.

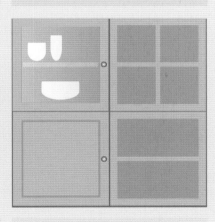

desk lamps

The best examples echo the workmanlike shapes and proportions of the original angled desk lamp designed in 1934. They work equally well as table lamps, bedside lights, task lighting, and, with special bases, floor lamps.

café furniture

Based on an original Spanish design, these chairs and tables are seen in coffee shops the world over. Cheaper versions are appearing in chains stores. Perfect for outdoors, they also look good in a modern kitchen.

modular components

Some are a variation on the simple cube storage systems of the early 1960s, while others are more sophisticated modular systems, poaching ideas from Jean Prouvé and Charles and Ray Eames.

5 good buys—low cost, high style

It's not only what you buy, but how you use it that turns an inexpensive piece of furniture into a stylish item. There are plenty of no-nonsense, cheap products around, and they often work better if you use several together in a row or other formal arrangement. Keep things simple by choosing plain shapes and solid colors. Avoid anything that looks flimsy, and don't mix too many different styles and materials.

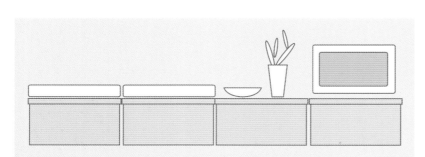

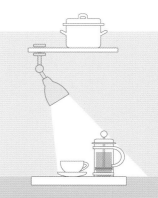

wooden boxes

Some home centers and large furniture chains sell a good selection of low-cost, stout, solid wooden-lidded boxes, ready for staining or painting. They are, of course, great for storage, but can also become an attractive piece of furniture in their own right.

Not only do they provide ample hidden storage; they can also double as a table, a seat, or a useful surface for anything from the TV to a collection of precious objects. Several of these boxes, placed side by side along a wall, are a cheap alternative to modular storage, with the advantage that you can choose both the color and finish.

clip-on lamps

Sophisticated lighting systems are expensive, as they require a qualified specialist to install wires and fittings. Clip-on lamps are no trouble at all, needing only a nearby outlet and a safe place where they can be securely clipped on. Use as task lights over a work surface or desk or as display lighting aimed at a picture or object. Turn toward the ceiling or wall to provide subtle background lighting.

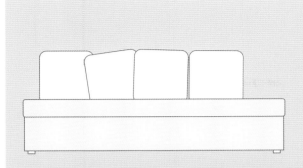

box springs

A new, narrow box spring can be picked up for a song in furniture stores and makes a great sofa, studio couch, and, when required, a spare bed. Don't just throw a bedspread over it, though, or it will look like an ordinary bed. Instead, layer the box spring with throws, and load it with scatter cushions. Alternatively, make a smart tailored cover or a fun frilly one.

Put two box springs together to make a swish-looking corner seating system—normally an expensive item. If you want your box spring to function well as a sofa, invest in some good-quality back cushions.

multiple pendant lampshades

Some of these lampshades are so inexpensive that you can buy three of them for less than the price of a single more expensive version. Why not hang three or more in rows above a dining table? Alternatively, hang a single lampshade low over a table in a sparely furnished room.

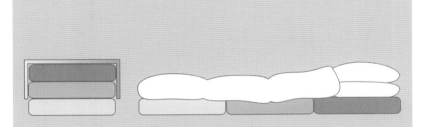

box cushions

Large, soft floor cushions are great for lolling around on, but they clutter up the space and are not much use for anything else. The newer box cushions are neater, smarter, and more versatile. Some are made of firm foam and look good in plain covers, whereas others are stuffed with feathers or constructed like mattresses and are often corded around the edges. These are more expensive, but three of them will probably still cost a lot less than a good quality stool, chair, or bed.

Pile up a stack of three cushions to make a footstool for weary feet or an extra seat.

A coordinating tray top is sometimes sold along with the cushions. Stack your cushions and add the tray top to transform them into an occasional table.

Spread them on the floor, and you have a comfortable, instant guest bed.

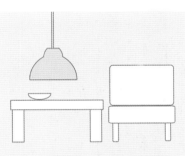

pendant lampshades

With an opaque metal shade, light escapes only at the base, throwing a pool of directional light. Stainless steel is cool and modern, but white and colored enamel can be perfect in a retro or more casual environment. Translucent glass throws light out of the sides as well as the base, providing more diffuse light. Plain white-etched glass suits any style and won't detract from the decor.

buying new shelving

Open shelves are an easy and efficient way of storing and displaying anything from books and saucepans to computers and clothes. Wall-mounted shelving systems are inexpensive and very versatile, but for those who can't or won't drill into walls, there are plenty of freestanding versions. Choose from wood, laminate, metal, and glass to create any number of looks, from rustic to sleek. Shelves will look good only if the contents are neatly or well displayed. Piles of junk just won't do, so be disciplined, and use your creative instincts to create a good impression.

shelf ideas

wall-mounted

The simple metal upright and bracket shelving systems illustrated are readily available and inexpensive. They are easy to put up, robust, versatile, and suitable for a variety of uses and locations, from hidden-away storage to open display.

Available in white, black, or silver metal finish, the uprights come in several heights with a range of bracket sizes for different widths of shelves. They can be configured to any size and can easily be made to fit exactly into alcoves and recesses. The height of the shelves can be adjusted to accommodate both short and tall objects. A small range of fittings are available, including dividers and end sections to prevent objects from toppling over or falling off the sides.

The largest brackets available will support a shelf deep enough to use as a work surface. Kitchen countertops, either wooden or laminate, work well but are heavy, so add extra support using screw-on legs. Packets or cans of food, utensils, and dishes can look attractive, especially when displayed in neat rows, storage jars, or hanging from hooks screwed to the underside of the shelves. Not everything looks good on show, so stow any unsightly things away behind a curtain hung from the countertop: this is a good way of disguising washing machines and dishwashers.

This type of shelving is also perfect for an instant, practical workstation, which can be used on its own or as part of a run of shelves in a kitchen, bedroom, living room, or even hallway.

For a bedroom, you can fashion shelves into a dressing table with extra storage. Stow away clothes and accessories in good-looking boxes, which keep everything clean and dust free. Pretty it up with paint, a gathered skirt, and an upholstered stool.

freestanding

Before fixing any shelves, make sure your walls can take the weight. Books, in particular, are very heavy, so make sure your hardware can stand the strain. If your walls aren't up to it, or if you can't or aren't allowed to drill into them, there are plenty of freestanding shelving systems and bookcases in a wide range of materials, dimensions, and configurations.

Some of the cheapest systems consist of wooden uprights with the shelves suspended between. They can look a bit utilitarian but are easily smartened up with paint or stain. If you like the industrial look, opt for galvanized versions, usually meant for garages and utility rooms.

Freestanding bookshelves in laminate are very inexpensive, and provided you use them confidently, preferably in rows of two or more, they look fine once they are filled up. Solid wood bookcases can be stained, painted, or polished, and if you want to hide things away for aesthetic or practical purposes, you could rig up a roller shade or, for a cozy look, a floral print curtain.

laminated board

The cheapest shelving option, consisting of particleboard with a laminated coating, usually in white, and available in a variety of widths. For a smarter, more sophisticated look, fix a piece of wood battening across the front of the shelves using finishing nails, then paint or stain to fit in with the rest of your decor.

chunky wood

For a more substantial look, buy thick planks from a lumberyard or home center. Sand down to a smooth finish, and paint or stain.

driftwood

There is no law that says shelves have to match, so use a collection of reclaimed planks, driftwood, or lucky dumpster finds to create something completely unique.

ready-made shelves

Some retailers sell shelving system components separately. So save money on expensive uprights by buying just the ready-made shelves in a style, material, and finish that would otherwise be unavailable or difficult to achieve.

small cabinets

Incorporate small wall cabinets into a shelving system to provide concealed storage for less attractive things, or, if you choose glass doors, an opportunity to display something precious.

buying new cheapskate choice

Thrift furniture can sometimes require a little alternative thinking. A separate work surface placed on top of filing cabinets provides not only a desk with plenty of useful storage, but an opportunity to choose materials tailored to your requirements and available space. Mass-market stores and office suppliers have affordable filing cabinets, but you could also use secondhand ones, painted if necessary. Surfaces can vary from a wooden tabletop or door to a laminated worktop. Scour home centers for other items, such as garden furniture, that can be adapted for indoor use.

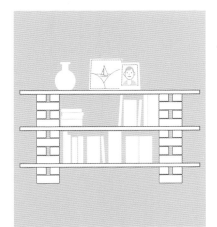

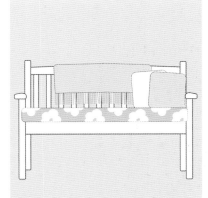

planks on bricks

A good thrift idea and perfect for the "industrial" look, especially if you use scaffolding planks. Once a cliché, this simple construction is back in fashion. It doesn't need to be fixed to the wall, but stability is crucial, so make sure you use enough bricks to form a stable construction. Bricks are heavy, so if you are worried about the floor, just build a low unit.

picnic bench

Extremely good value for very little money and available at many home centers, as well as garden centres. Paint in thick gloss paint, and use as seating in a kitchen diner. For extra comfort, put cushions on the bench seats. These benches are quite wide so may not be suitable for very cramped spaces.

garden bench

Plain wooden garden benches can be turned into indoor seating with a coat of paint and some seat cushions. Besides looking good, extra cushions or draped throws and quilts provide added comfort. Perfect for a summery, seashore feel and great in kitchens.

10 picture ideas

clip joint

Clip frames can look cheap, so glam them up by framing the picture within a large border using special paper. Try handmade, textured papers or very beautiful art paper.

old prints

Look in secondhand bookstores and specialist art booksellers for old exhibition catalogs, which are usually very inexpensive and supply good-quality reproductions for framing.

plain and simple

Simple aluminum or black frames look very discreet and are perfect for black-and-white photographs or drawings.

keep it simple

Sticking to a single style of frame will unify a mixture of prints, paintings, and photographs.

single line

A single row of pictures set halfway up the wall looks sophisticated. You don't have to keep to one size, but hang the pictures with all tops or all bottoms toeing the line.

sight lines

When hanging pictures, don't hang them too high, or you won't be able to appreciate them properly. Work out the best position to view a picture from a seated as well as a standing position.

off the wall

Propping pictures against the wall gives you a different vantage point and saves making holes in the wall. Useful for covering electrical plugs, cables, and unsightly floor-level holes or stains.

well planned

A satisfying arrangement of pictures takes time and considerable trial and error. Use the drawing program on your PC to plot the positions of pictures on a scale drawing, and save your wall from unnecessary holes.

keep control

Don't dot pictures around the place. Lining them up in disciplined rows or containing them within just one wall will give them greater impact.

shelf life

A narrow shelf is a great way to display pictures. Now widely available in wood or metal, they avoid the need for hanging; just prop up the pictures and change them around whenever you like.

lighting

When it comes to lighting, limited resources do not mean limited options, as the range available is huge, and much of it remarkably inexpensive. The problem may be that, faced with an abundance of styles, colors, and finishes, you can easily get carried away. You are more likely to throw good light on your surroundings if you curb your enthusiasm and adopt a disciplined approach. For best results, especially in a small or open-plan home, keep to one or two styles. But you don't have to be well behaved all the time, so add some pizzazz with a chandelier or colored light show.

general illumination

Spotlights and downlighters give overall illumination. Styles vary from standard spotlights, available singly or in rows or groups of three or more, to adventurous, curved metal shapes. Recessed downlighters are popular for living areas and kitchens, look modern, and give an overall wash of light, but not all ceilings are suited to these. The system, which usually operates at a different voltage and requires a separate circuit, should be installed by a professional. A good system is expensive, but can be worth the investment.

The interest in retro furnishings has led to a reappraisal of the single, central ceiling light, with drum shades, glass shaded light fixtures and chandeliers back in favor. If your central light is used only occasionally, it will look fine with a plain frosted glass, fabric, or paper shade.

pendant lights

A longer cord on a ceiling light makes it a pendant. To save the expense of moving a light fixture, use a long cord looped through a hook screwed into the ceiling, and hang the light wherever you want it. A paper lantern hung low in a corner looks good. Rows of pendant lights look trendy and are a good alternative to spotlights or downlighters in a kitchen.

wall lights

Much subtler than overhead lighting. Some require wiring into the wall, which could be an expensive bother, but there are plug-in versions too. Single plug-in spotlights fixed in a row halfway up the wall are cheap and easy to do and can be angled to create a variety of effects.

task lighting

Desk lamps provide good illumination for reading, knitting, and even cooking, but can also be angled to give general light. Floor lamps can be placed next to a chair or desk, doubling as spotlights. Keep an eye out for older versions and for new aluminum photographers' lamps, which are both cheap and stylish.

lamp bases and floor lamps

With the wide range of shades available, it is possible to create any style, from antique and retro to minimalist and modern. Slim metal lamp bases complement most interior styles, but ceramic lamp bases are back in fashion in all guises from fancy urns to matte, solid-colored glazes. Old, turned, wooden lamp bases often turn up in secondhand stores; they can be stripped and polished or painted to be used with either a modern, plain drum shade or a pretty, patterned shade, for a nostalgic effect. Make your own lamps using a lamp fitting available from home centers and electrical retailers. Be daringly kitsch and use a Chianti bottle, or terribly arty and use a glass bowl filled with pebbles or marbles.

display lighting

Plug-in downlighters with their own transformers can be fixed underneath shelves and inside cabinets to highlight your possessions. Picture lights were once considered passé, but if you have a stunning image, why not make the most of it?

feature lights

Christmas tree lights, or versions of them, are easy to plug in and provide limitless possibilities. String them along shelves or behind beds, or hang them across walls.

stow away

chests, boxes, and trunks

One large chest can hold a lot of stuff
and be used as a seat, table, or surface
for display. Ideal for linens and clothes,
but keep moths at bay with lavender or
old-fashioned mothballs. Also great for
stowing unsightly equipment and tools.
Give beautiful examples pride of place;
disguise the more prosaic with a coat
of paint or a colorful throw.

bags and baskets

Many of us have a weakness for bags
and can't resist buying more. Use them
for storage, hang them up Shaker-style
on hooks, or arrange them decoratively
on shelves, floors, or tops of
cupboards. Good for anything, including
laundry, gloves, socks and shoes,
scarves, pantyhose, towels, and toys.

suitcases and hampers

Old cases aren't great for taking on
vacation but they are perfect for storing
anything from clothes to photographs.
While old ones have charm, new cases
can be very chic. Decant their contents
into plastic garbage bags when you
need them for trips away.

storage

Whether you want to keep things safe, clean, or out of sight or just like to know where everything is, storage is an important issue for every interior. Lots of storage ideas are discussed throughout this book, but there is always room for another idea and an alternative approach, so here are a few more.

clear out

Storage can be a big problem, but it is also big business. There is no shortage of storage "solutions" available that promise to bring stylish order to our lives. But before you give in to temptation and buy a huge quantity of beautiful boxes or baskets, think carefully. Some so-called storage solutions often take up a lot of room and can become a storage problem in themselves, as well as encouraging us to keep things that would be better thrown away.

De-cluttering is not only fashionable but a good way of reducing storage needs by weeding out the unloved, unattractive, and unnecessary, leaving only what you want and need.

closets

If your existing closet space is ample for your storage needs, you're lucky! Most people could do with a bit more—for shoes, handbags, suitcases, out-of-season clothing, sports equipment, and other cumbersome items. If, after throwing out unwanted items, you still can't shut the closet doors, the next step is to reorganize. You can buy and install a closet organizing system that will use the space more efficiently. Or you could get a carpenter to fit a system of shelves and extra rails tailored to your own requirements, which might not cost much more than a ready-made system.

built-in storage

Still need more storage? The solution might be to build an additional closet within the bedroom itself. This approach works best if you can devote the better part of a wall—or even a whole wall—to closets, or a mixture of closets, cabinets, and drawers. In this way the system will look like an integral part of the room, rather tahn an afterthought. To offset the loss of floor sace, you could have one cr more closet doors faced with a full-length mirror.

A similar approach can be used to provide storage in a living room or den, using a combination of cabinets, shelves, and/or drawers. Shelves are cheaper than cabinets, but not everyone wants to see what is on them.

Whatever type of system you're planning, remember that it will be a major focal point and that bad workmanship will be highly visible. If you can't afford to pay for a good job, some freestanding storage furniture is a better choice.

cupboards and armoires

A good-sized freestanding cupboard can hold a huge amount of stuff, especially if you fit it with some shelves and cubbyholes. The kind used in schools and offices can sometimes be bought secondhand. Wardrobes, or armoires, traditionally used for clothing, can be converted for storing all sorts of items. Antique armoires in good condition fetch high prices, but one in bad repair might, with a little TLC, be rendered useful and even handsome.

keep on display

If something is beautiful or even just pleasing to the eye, display it. In a kitchen it is far easier to pick a mug off a hook or a plate off a plate rack or dresser than delve into a cabinet. Books and magazines are more likely to be read if they are kept on open shelves or are piled on a table or the floor.

practical projects

If you have taken stock of what you've got and decided to make the most of your home and its contents, now is the time to make good the basic structure. Set in motion a program of repairs and refinements that will provide a solid foundation for any finishing interior flourishes and show off your treasures in the best possible way.

building basics

A comprehensive tour of your home will help to assess where your priorities lie. Your tight budget may be used up with mundane repairs, but it will be a worthwhile investment. All properties respond to a little TLC—a programme of hole filling, surface smoothing, and other basic repairs, followed by a coat of paint, has been known to produce silk purses from sows' ears and will generate the feel-good factor.

Zoning regulations, building codes, and health and safety matters apply to even minor building works. Any violations of rules or mistakes in calculations are potentially dangerous, against the law, and very expensive. Before embarking on any work, it is advisable, and often essential, to employ an expert, in the form of an architect or structural engineer. Choose carefully—contact the relevant organizations, including your local authority, for recommended contractors— and ask to check contractors' credentials. Building work can be the stuff of nightmares, but the pain will be lessened if you use a reputable contractor, know exactly what the work entails and what to expect, and have a basic knowledge of how it is to be done. This is where an expert comes in handy—some even offer to supervise the work for a fee. Though expensive, this fee could save you money and time lost through mistakes, misunderstandings, and mishaps.

cost analysis

Those on a tight budget often dismiss thoughts of structural or refurbishment work, fearing that the costs are way above their means. However, small-scale works with a large impact can cost hundreds rather than thousands.

expensive
Major building works need the services of an architect, structural engineer, and good building contractors, as well as the approval of the local authorities.

Leave electrical work and plumbing to professionals, as they involve pulling up floors and knocking holes in walls.

not as expensive as you think
Plastering and skimming should definitely be done by an expert. Although it makes a mess, it doesn't take long. Smooth walls and ceilings make a huge difference to the quality of a decorative scheme.

New floors may cause considerable disruption when laid, but a professional job by a specialist can give a dramatic effect and be well worth the expense.

Small building works, such as taking down an interior wall or building a new one, are relatively easy and surprisingly inexpensive.

very reasonable
Paint can completely transform a room, and your life, for very little cost.

New fixtures and cabinets can be excellent value, are often well designed, and come in huge ranges, including lighting, bathroom fixtures, and storage solutions.

free
All that you need is your labor and that of friends and family, enthusiasm, and imagination.

schedule of works

Armed with a clipboard, go around your home and assess its condition. Note anything that needs attention, repair, removal, or reappraisal. Poke into every corner—including the roof space, if possible—and under flooring and wallcoverings to examine the state of walls, ceilings, floors, windows, doors, and any built-in fixtures.

structure

Is your home structurally sound? If necessary, hire someone to check for infestations of termites, powder post beetle, or fungal attack; this last is common in moist climates and causes wood decay, also called dry rot. Have a good poke around; if you have access to the roof space, check joists and roof timbers, looking for evidence of damage.

floors

Take up any flooring to inspect the floors, noting any damage, damp, and suitability for treatment. You never know, you may find wonderful wood, beautiful tiles, or trendy lino gasping for air. Are the floorboards good enough to strip, or are they better covered up? Can old parquet floors be revived? With solid floors, is the subfloor OK? Can tiles be repaired/replaced? Can holes be filled, or is something more drastic required?

walls and ceilings

Tap surfaces to check for holes and hidden damage. Is the surface in good condition? If not, can it be put right with filler or does it need replastering? Does wallpaper need removing, or can it be painted or papered over?

woodwork

Check door frames, picture rails, moldings, and baseboards. Do they need rubbing down or stripping? If they are in poor condition, will a coat of paint suffice? Can they be repaired, or would it be easier to replace them?

built-in furniture

Strip out any built-in cabinets and shelves that are badly made, too far gone to repair, or just ugly.

windows

Do they fit? Are they in good condition? Do they need replacing or just minor repairs, plus a good rub down, a coat of paint, and new hardware? Are they secure? Time to put in patio doors or French windows?

doors

Do they fit and open and close properly? Do they need replacing? Do they need to be there? Would they be better hung the other way around? Would glass bring in more light? How are you going to treat them—strip, rub down, paint?

electrical supply

Is it safe? Do you have the latest fuse box? Do you know your circuits? Do you want to put in track lighting (in which case you will need a new circuit) or new wiring for sound or communication systems. Do you want to reroute wiring and cables so that they are safer and/or out of sight?

plumbing

Locate the main shutoff valve; and make sure you know where the pipes are. Do you want to relocate the supply or drainage?

gas

Never touch anything to do with gas yourself. Get gas appliances checked regularly by a registered expert.

heating/air conditioning

Inspect the current system for faults or leaks. Do you want to install a new type of heating?

energy eco-check

Insulation saves energy. Is your system efficient? Are there eco-alternatives?

health and safety

Do you have a smoke alarm? If not, get one now. They are cheap and easy to install. Do you have proper ventilation for gas appliances? An expert will check.

structural sense

Just as an expensive outfit is spoiled by scruffy shoes, shabby rooms detract from even the most beautiful furniture. In the priority stakes, you might be better to opt for a beautiful floor and fewer furnishings.

floors

If you want the stripped bare look, make sure the surface is sealed to minimize wear and keep out dirt and stains (see page opposite). If you have live woodworm or other suspected pests, seek advice and treat as necessary.

Stone and tiled floors respond well to a good clean: rent an industrial machine for such a tough job, then seal with a proprietary sealant or wax polish. A few small defects in a stone floor add to its character, but missing tiles are not so charming. If replacement tiles are available, use them to fill in any gaps. If not, use heavy-duty filler or concrete mix.

Bare concrete can be a much smarter alternative to worn carpet or vile vinyl, but it must be sealed to keep in potentially harmful dust. Give the floor a good scrub, fill in any cracks and holes, then coat with a clear sealant or floor paint.

Good-quality carpet is worth keeping, and if it is not too threadbare or stained, industrial cleaning works wonders. If you are taking up your carpet, avoid too much waste by cutting up any good pieces and making them into rugs. The edges need to be cut very neatly, but would look better still trimmed with carpet or binding tape.

Old linoleum and vinyl complement the fashionable retro look. They can be given a new lease on life with a good scrub and a coating of sealant or polish.

walls

If you think your bare plaster can pass muster as "delightfully distressed" then leave your walls alone. Otherwise, even out any holes with an all-purpose filler, then replaster or skim, if necessary. Don't worry too much about uneven surfaces; small defects won't show under a couple of coats of paint or wallpaper.

woodwork

Damaged window frames, moldings, and baseboards can spoil an otherwise attractive interior. Smaller defects can be repaired using wood filler but more severe damage may require a patch using a matching molding.

New moldings and baseboards pull a room together and do not cost very much. For a crisp, clean look use square-edged lengths of wood—deep and chunky, if you like.

windows

The style and state of the windows have a huge effect on an interior scheme. Original windows obviously look best, as they were designed to complement the architectural style and proportions of the building. Poor-quality or inappropriate replacement windows can seriously affect the value of your house. Sensible and sensitive owners are taking them out and reverting to architecturally correct, period style or good-quality new equivalents. If you don't own your house or apartment, or changing windows is too expensive, disguise them with shutters, blinds, metal mesh, or wooden or fabric screens.

doors

New doors are not expensive, but don't go for the ready-finished variety, they look cheap. Traditional paneled designs suit older properties, but flat, flush finishes give a more modern look. If the doors are an important architectural feature of your house and have been removed or defaced, save up for the real thing from salvage yards or specialist dealers. If your house is old but the doors are flat, rather than paneled, they may have been covered in plywood in the 1950s or '60s. It's worth checking.

5 frugal floors

stripped

One of the easiest ways to smarten a room is to strip existing floorboards and seal them with paint, varnish, wax, or oil. If the boards are in good shape and a pleasing color, a matte varnish will give a warm yet clean look. For a dramatic statement, use a dark or colored stain—exercise caution, however, as it can be oppressive. Floor paint is now available in a wide range of colors. Although some ranges are expensive, they do give a dense, smooth finish that will cover most imperfections.

particleboard/MDF

Often used as an underlayment for resilient flooring, particleboard can, in a pinch, be used on its own—perhaps as a temporary measure if you can't yet afford the top-quality linoleum you've set your heart on, Medium density fiberboard (MDF) can also be used in this way. Either should be sealed with varnish or paint. It can be laid directly onto the existing subfloor, but a layer of polystyrene underneath will provide some insulation of heat and sound.

laminated

This easy-to-lay flooring is very popular and has helped provide homes across the land with the "light and airy" feel. Some are extremely cheap, but be careful as the surface is rarely real wood, instead it is a photograph printed onto laminate, which, while convincing, will wear off in areas of high traffic in a relatively short time. Also, floors need to breathe, and many people have discovered that underneath a "well-fitted" laminate floor, condensation has rotted the joists.

tiles

The advantage of tiles is that they are extremely hard-wearing and therefore a thrifty option. Also, the development of thinner tiles makes them easier to cut and lay, and flexible grouting means that a concrete subfloor is no longer essential. There is a huge variety available, including stone and slate, traditional quarry tiles, and plain or decorated ceramic.

carpet

Wall-to-wall carpet is often the cheapest and most sensible option; fortunately, it is back in fashion. Not only does it cover a multitude of sins, it is also warm and absorbs sound. Stick to solid, neutral colors. Sea-grass, Sisal, and other natural fibers are usually more expensive and need to be stuck down, adding to the expense; also they hold dirt and can't be cleaned as easily as a pile carpet.

prudent decorator

Providing you don't go in for too many specialist paints or particularly swanky wallpaper, decorating need not be an expensive business. Prudent painters use color and a clean background as a basis for thrifty good looks.

preparation

The toughest and most tedious part of decorating is the preparation. The time and effort invested in preparing surfaces and woodwork are rewarded with a finish that not only looks better but last longer.

Walls and ceilings that are in good condition require only a quick dust down. If they are very dirty, or covered in remnants of wallpaper, they should be washed down with a warm, mild solution of detergent, followed by plain water. Woodwork should be rubbed down using abrasive paper or washed with de-greaser to break down the hard surface and provide a "tooth" for the new coat of paint.

You can save money and effort by leaving any woodwork unpainted. Some evidence of age, including chips and flakes, can be attractive, but dirty and tacky paintwork is not. Wash woodwork down to remove any fingermarks and goo.

Untreated wood and metal need to be given a coat of primer before painting. This protects the material and provides a good base for paint. The available range of primers has expanded to include those suitable for shiny surfaces, such as melamine. These are perfect for the thrifty, as they enable you to paint over kitchen cabinets, tiles, and any items finished with a hard, shiny varnish.

paint points

Buy your paints from one of the large manufacturers—they are often cheaper, and the colors are helpfully grouped to make selection easier. Normally, latex flat paint is used on walls, with gloss or eggshell on woodwork. Modern latex paints, especially the washable varieties, can also be used on woodwork that is not exposed to high wear.

Available in a flat or semi gloss finish, latex paint is water-based and therefore easy to apply. Gloss paint dries to a hard, shiny finish; it is more viscous and consequently trickier to use. Gloss is very hard-wearing and lasts a long time, so unless you want to change the color, it won't always have to be redone every time you redecorate. Eggshell, or satin finish, paint has a softer, more matte finish and is easier to apply than gloss, but is not so hard-wearing. Traditionally, gloss and eggshell paints have been solvent-based, which made them smelly and a potential health hazard. These paints are now being phased out, and water-based, low VOCs (volatile organic compounds) versions introduced, which are more pleasant to use and dry much more quickly.

posh paint

Some specialist paint ranges include the most wonderful colors and give a distinctly different finish. If paint is your passion, it may well be worth the extra expense. Architecturally beautiful houses should always be treated with respect; and besides being historically correct, some of these paints will enhance a building's appearance.

wallpaper

The good news is that wallpaper—perfect for covering poor, uneven surfaces—is back in fashion. The bad news is that the best papers are very expensive. Thrifty options include papering just one wall, finding a lucky bargain in a sale, or using a cheaper paper. This third option is tricky as it is difficult to find good cheap papers. The once-despised palm fronds and sprigged flowers came back into fashion just as they were being banished from the ranges of the mass-market producers and retailers. Unfortunately they have been repackaged as trendy, with a higher price tag.

stencil

A cheaper way to cover a wall with pattern is stenciling. Avoid anything sentimental or complicated. Exercise subtlety with simple designs and tones of one color, or a family of colors, rather than a whole paintbox.

get creative

Plain walls are all very well, but occasionally you may desire something a bit different, so don't hold back. Indulge your creative urges and get arty; or, if you're more pragmatic, use the wall as an extra storage or display area.

memory lane

Turn one wall into a giant scrapbook—the perfect place for all those cutouts you've never gotten around to putting in a proper book. Do the same with your favorite photographs and postcards. Depending on the state of the wall, stick them up with tacks or adhesive putty, but try to maintain some sort of order and method to stop it from looking a mess.

mapped out

Maps are large, colorful, and fairly cheap. They are also informative and offer the opportunity to brush up on your geography, plan a trip, or study a place you know and love. World maps tend to be brightly colored with lots of blue sea, but for a more sophisticated effect choose the subtle green tones of a Geological Survey map.

museum piece

Don't hide your treasures away. Whether they are china dogs, stamps, model airplanes, or driftwood, get out your cherished collections and put them where you can admire them. An edited selection will look chic, but why not go that little bit further and cover an entire wall with a display using shelves or glass-fronted cabinets. They don't need to match.

hang it all

Wall hangings are great decoration and conveniently cover up poor or unattractive surfaces. They can add character to a plain room as well as a bit of extra warmth. What you hang on your wall depends on what you've got—it could be a rug, dhurrie, kilim, embroidered panel, piece of appliqué or patchwork, or just a piece of nice fabric. It can be homemade or something picked up in a souk, ethnic shop, or furniture superstore.

hang-ups

Do the Shaker thing, and fix a row of pegs around your walls to hang your chairs upon. This keeps the floor clear for that uncluttered look. The chairs will, of course, stick out into the room, so if space is very limited, use folding chairs. Add a folding table, and you could hang up a whole dining suite.

kitchens culinary choice

The thrift philosophy involves prioritizing, so the amount you spend on your kitchen should be determined by how much time you spend in it and how it fits in to your lifestyle. Installing a brand-new kitchen is a major expense, so think hard before making any decisions. Freshly painted walls, new ceramic tiles, and a revived floor—which would be included in most new schemes anyway—might just be enough to give the existing kitchen a new lease on life.

top priority

If the kitchen really is the heart of your home, be prepared to lavish the majority of your budget on this one room. Spend wisely, taking time and getting advice on the best way to do so.

If you do a lot of cooking, put an oven, work surfaces, and storage at the top of your priority list. If you do tear out your old kitchen, avoid replacing it with a cheap option because generally they aren't terribly robust—edges, trims, and hinges will soon show signs of wear. Go for cabinets in solid wood or high-quality laminates with good carcasses, hinges, runners, doors, and drawer hardware.

If you entertain a lot, or have a big family, a huge side-by-side refrigerator, with masses of freezer space, an ice-cube maker, and all the other refinements, may be a good investment. Otherwise, a normal-size model will meet your needs. Similarly, a state-of-the-art range, with two ovens, is superfluous if you live on takeouts.

fast food

If you are a busy person with no interest in cooking, who seldom entertains at home and uses the kitchen only for hot drinks and serving up takeouts, inexpensive cabinets will suffice, as they won't be subjected to intense wear. Go for a small, galley-style kitchen or a minimalist kitchen housed along one wall to free up space for other purposes.

Lifestyles and circumstances do change, however, so if you think you are likely to spend more time in the kitchen in the future, make allowances and invest in something altogether more hard-wearing and hardworking.

layout

There are lots of rules on kitchen layouts involving work triangles and what or what not to put where, but rooms and lives are not always quite so standardized. The layout of a kitchen will be determined to a great extent on the space available and the position of any plumbing, windows, and doors. Kitchen suppliers will plan your room for you, but don't assume they know best—their job is to sell cabinets, and they often overprescribe in the storage department. If your want your kitchen to be a sociable area, it may be better to have fewer cabinets, in favor of a large table, which serves as work surface and storage, as well as entertaining.

materials

Advanced production techniques and an expanding market have made materials that were once deemed luxury, and therefore expensive, widely available at realistic prices. Materials such as limestone, slate, and terrazzo are now available in thinner tiles suitable for walls, countertops, and floors. Convincing imitations of these luxury materials, in the form of ceramic tiles and laminates, are now also widespread.

Likewise, new manufacturing processes have also placed solid wooden countertops within range of smaller budgets. Providing you treat them regularly with oil, they will last for years. The disadvantage of laminated units has always been the edges, where poor joins and a tendency to chip eventually show up their shortcomings. New techniques for spray-coating fiberboards now give a better, longer-lasting finish. Etched glass looks sophisticated and modern and is being used very successfully even at the cheaper end of the market.

5 thrifty tips

A new layout doesn't have to mean throwing everything out and starting again. Faced with a kitchen full of cabinets that aren't in the best state of repair, why not redesign the space using only the good stuff and then smarten it all up with new countertop?

A good-quality countertop may cost more but can make ordinary cabinets look expensive. Likewise, it can pull a motley collection of cabinets and appliances into some sort of order.

Fix a long metal pole to the wall or spanning the width of a narrow kitchen or alcove. Then buy a batch of butchers' hooks and hang up all your pots, pans, utensils, and sundry items.

Hooks are cheap, and a row of them is ideal for dish towels, aprons, shopping bags, coats, dog leashes, and other paraphernalia. Hanging bags and baskets also provide extra space for storage.

If you can't afford or don't want base cabinets, a curtain will hide appliances and open shelves. Gathered gingham or a flowery print will look either nostalgic or downright pretty, while plain or striped linen or cotton, ungathered, with eyelets and threaded onto a metal pole will look minimalist and modern.

kitchens door handles

It's a relatively easy decision to replace a kitchen that is in bad repair and doesn't meet your needs for storage and layout, but what do you do if the existing cabinets are in fine fettle, but just look tired and dated? Ripping out a perfectly good kitchen is wasteful, as well as ecologically unsound, but it is possible to revive and restore doors and drawer fronts with paint or stain and by adding new handles and knobs.

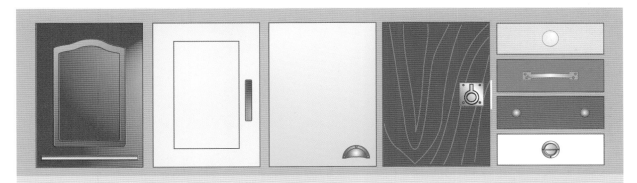

doors and drawers

There are a number of new primers available, which ensure that paint will stick to shiny, non-porous surfaces. This means you can even paint over laminates. A facelift will work well only if you take care to do a good paint job. Before painting, take off all hinges and handles, and don't forget to do both sides.

You can update old solid wooden cabinets with a dramatic dark stain, but you will have to sand off any varnish and take great care not to get a patchy look.

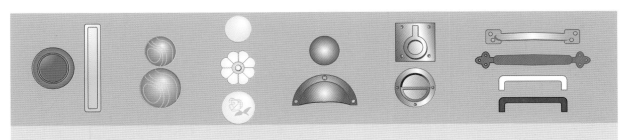

knobs and handles

Choose from a huge range from the large home centers and furniture stores, as well as specialist stores. Removing old handles will leave holes in the doors and drawers, so your choice of replacement and where you position them may be restricted.

Besides modern and minimalist—which will add class to dull cabinets—look for retro plastic or chunky rustic handles. Dare to be different, with decorated porcelain or antique knobs. Simple metal pull handles and locker fittings will look shipshape.

kitchens alternative remedies

Although standard built-in kitchens are neat and efficient, they can lack character, and sometimes they just don't suit your taste, lifestyle, house, or the space available. In addition, drilling into walls may not be an option if the walls are uneven, not strong enough, or too nice to cover up. An alternative is the eclectic European-style kitchen, which you create yourself. This approach gives you the opportunity to make up your own idiosyncratic style using a mixture of furniture, fixtures, and finds garnered from bargain-hunting forays, new pieces, and inherited favorites. Take a new look at what is available and use a bit of ingenuity and flair, plus perhaps a coat of paint to put together something a little bit different, which needn't cost the earth.

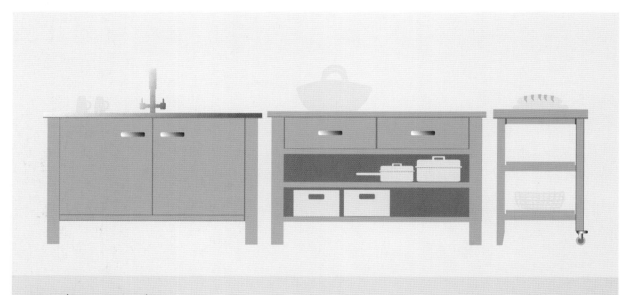

separate components

The great economical advantage of an eclectic kitchen is that you can take it with you when you move.
What's more, you don't have to drill any holes into your walls, or even have good walls, and you can move the furniture around to suit any changing circumstances or on a whim.

An added bonus is that an eclectic kitchen can be added to over a period of time, as and when you can afford it.

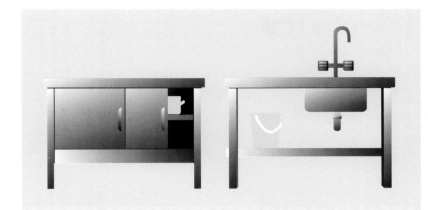

catering

Stainless-steel, high-quality catering fixtures cost a fraction of the price of the domestic versions. They are normally of a very practical and unfussy design, but bear in mind that they are for use in restaurant and school kitchens, so they are quite large. Buy new direct from catering suppliers—you may have to persuade them to accept a small order—or buy old from secondhand furniture and office suppliers. Use the Internet for sources.

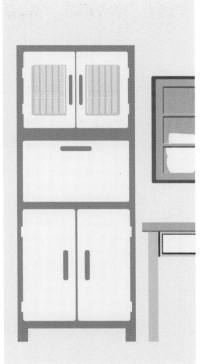

lockers

Fitting lots of smaller cupboards avoids wasting any space, as well as cutting down the time spent rummaging around at the back of large cabinets for lost ingredients. Lockers make an unusual and efficient alternative to standard kitchen cabinets. They tend to be narrower than standard cabinets, so they make good use of small spaces. You can buy them new from specialist retailers, where you will be able to choose from a range of colors; or keep a lookout for old office and school equipment.

serendipity

Choosing separate kitchen furnishings makes for a more personal, characterful, and possibly cheaper decorating scheme. Chests of drawers, large cupboards, and dressers are all great for storage. One large cupboard can house everything including pots, pans, china, equipment, and food. An unused chest of drawers is great for storing a wide variety of stuff, from "unruly" ingredients, such as packets of rice, pulses, and pasta, to children's notebooks and crayons.

kitchens plus

Changing lifestyles and the high premium on space have led to changes in how rooms are allocated and used. A tendency toward fewer, bigger rooms, rather than several small ones, has meant less activity-specific areas and more multifunctional areas, such as great rooms. Kitchens are no longer just places for cooking or washing, but are used for paperwork and socializing, too.

+ dine

In a small kitchen, a fold-down table and a couple of stools hung on the wall will free up space for cooking but allow you to eat in comfort. A breakfast bar is easier to fit in and can be fixed at normal table or bar height. If there is no room for a farmhouse-scale table, opt for something long and narrow, and use benches instead of chairs.

+ live

Kitchens can be cozy, sociable places and the perfect place for a sofa, armchairs, the TV, and sound system. If space is a problem, it may be possible to squeeze in just one armchair (why not make it a rocking chair?), or build in a bench or window seat. Failing that, make dining chairs comfortable enough for prolonged stays.

+ work

A kitchen can be a good place for a bit of peace and quiet and the ideal environment in which to work, whether it's doing homework, paying the bills, or even earning your living. Such a workspace could be a table that doubles as a desk, a designated section of countertop with space underneath for a stool, or a whole mini-office in a converted armoire to protect computers and other equipment from steam. Even a fold-down table will provide enough space for a laptop computer.

+ play

Even if you have a large living room, the chances are that children will end up around your feet when you are in the kitchen. If you are knocking two rooms together, think about opening up or adding space next to the kitchen to create a play area where you can keep an eye on them while getting on with the chores. Penning small children in with a gate or low partition will keep them safe from the potential dangers of cooking and appliances.

+ active

For a kitchen that turns into a studio for painting, pottery, or other artistic pursuits, keep surfaces clear and easy to clean. A double sink minimizes the risk of unsuitable or dangerous ingredients entering the food chain. A large expanse of kitchen floor can be just the place for yoga or exercises. For less active pursuits, such as book club or committee meetings, a large kitchen table is ideal.

bathrooms freshen-ups

Design expectations in the bathroom area are much higher now than they used to be. Bringing a tired and not-very-hygienic-looking bathroom up to scratch doesn't have to be too expensive, providing your aim is for something pleasant and functional rather than hip and flashy.

coat of paint

If your bathroom floor, walls, and fixtures are in generally good condition, a coat of paint could be all that's needed to make the room look better, or even sensational. The bathroom is the one place eminently suited to the white-box treatment; a liberal application of brilliant white paint, which could also include the floor, will make the space look and feel fresh and hyper-hygienic. Alternatively, a small bathroom offers the opportunity to go mad and use intense colors.

accessorize

An obvious thrifty way to smarten up a lackluster but perfectly functional bathroom is with smart, matching accessories. Even the low-price chain stores and supermarkets sell good-quality ranges of plain bathroom accessories at bargain prices. A new bathroom tissue holder, towel rail, shower curtain, and toothbrush holder can work wonders, as can a new toilet seat, mirror, and medicine cabinet. For a modern look, stainless-steel and white-coated steel accessories work best. A cozy or nostalgic bathroom can cope with wood,

especially if it is painted. Look for small, pretty cabinets and shelves in flea markets and secondhand stores. Matching towels smarten up any bathroom, and there is no good excuse for holding back in this department, as these can be picked up at very low prices everywhere, including department stores, supermarkets, bed and bath stores, and market stalls.

irony

If you are stuck with hideous wall tiles or colored bathroom fixtures that refuse to look trendy, then go for excess. Make a virtue out of disadvantage, and celebrate those pink tiles with extra-fluffy pink towels, bathmat, and outrageous wallpaper, featuring cabbage roses or peonies. Don't forget to include the bathtub panel in the scheme of things.

small is affordable

A small space provides the chance to use luxurious materials that would be prohibitively expensive over a large area. Consider limestone, marble, or slate for floors as well as walls and other surfaces. One roll of expensive but exceptionally

beautiful wallpaper will be enough for a small bathroom, and the same goes for a specialist paint in that must-have color.

tile tips

Ceramic tiles are relatively inexpensive, providing you stick to plain ones. Putting them up yourself is a straightforward job, as long as you stick to thin tiles that can be easily cut. Taking off old tiles can be a difficult and messy business, but if you don't want the bother, you can add new tiles on top of the old. The grouting between tiles tends to become grubby over time, but applying new grouting is simple and cheap. If you want something different, use a contrasting color—white with dark tiles or a soft gray with white are both effective.

light effect

A distinctly average bathroom can be transformed with lighting, but safety is a key issue wherever electricity and water are concerned. Any new fixtures should be installed by an expert, which could be expensive but may still be cheaper than more drastic improvements. Good lighting is essential for makeup and shaving.

fresh start checklist

If your existing bathroom is beyond the pale, it is often easier to strip everything out and start again. Good-quality, well-designed, simple bathroom suites, comprising a toilet, sink , and bathtub, are surprisingly cheap, as are faucets and shower heads.

floor

Take up any old floor coverings and check for damp and rot. Bare boards can be painted using gloss or floor paint. A solid wood floor is fine, as long as it is sealed to prevent water damage, but wood laminates aren't good in a bathroom, as they will lift when wet. Tiles are good, and in a small space you can indulge in luxury limestone, slate, or ceramic. Vinyl is waterproof, but if you plan to install it yourself, cutting and laying it around the fixtures can be tricky. A concrete floor can be sealed and painted with floor paint.

walls

Before painting, papering, or tiling walls, seal any damp patches using a proprietary sealant. Satin-finish, semi-gloss, and gloss paints are waterproof, but any buildup of soap is not so easy to remove. Water-resistant, wipe-down wallpaper is quite thick and good for covering uneven or stained surfaces but may start to peel if ventilation is poor. Tiles are the perfect wall covering for bathrooms, especially showers. As long as you stick to solid-colored, slim tiles, the cost will not be too high, whereas backsplash panels are

sufficient for bathtubs and basins. Tiling all walls to backsplash height creates a very easy-to-clean, hygienic environment.

ventilation

If you have mold, mildew, or fungus, it is probably due to bad ventilation. Opening a window is sometimes enough, but you may need to install a fan or vent.

plumbing

Moving pipework is costly, but worth the expense if the new layout improves your home. Starting from scratch provides a good opportunity for rerouting and concealing pipework, as well as installing a new tub, shower, toilet, or extra sink.

shower versus bathtub

While some love a long soak in a bath, others prefer the convenience of a short shower. It is tempting to free up space in a small bathroom by dispensing with the bathtub, but think twice. There are times when a bath is best—bathing young children or soothing tired muscles, for example. When you come to sell your house, the absence of a bathtub could reduce its value. A shower over the tub is a good compromise, as long as you have a glass screen or generous shower

curtain to contain the water. Alternatively, consider a special small bathtub with a seat, which combines the activities of bathing and showering.

bathroom fixtures

White is best, and simple is better than fancy, especially if your budget is limited. Steel bathtubs are heavier and slightly more expensive than plastic, but they are a better buy, as they last longer and don't creak alarmingly when you climb in. Avoid fancy details, such as shell-shaped soap holders and ugly bathtub panels. Shower floors are normally sold separately and come in a range of sizes. Ceramic is easier to clean, but weight could be a problem.

fitting the bill

Super-sophisticated faucets and shower fittings can cost the earth, but there are good, well-designed, modern-looking taps available at modest prices. Or you could splash out on expensive fittings, the outlay won't be huge as you will only need one bathroom tissue holder, a few hooks, and one or more towel rails. Mirrors make a bathroom feel bigger and more glamorous. Large mirror panels are available in home centers.

furniture restore and repair

Old and not-so-old furniture benefits from a little tender loving care, being reborn as good as new or even in a different guise. Just a little damage can reduce the value of an item quite considerably, so if you have the time, skill, and patience to take on a restoration project, take advantage of the good bargains available.

Before buying anything, assess what you may be letting yourself in for. If the item in question is very beautiful, good quality, a rarity, or an antique and if you are handy with tools, you may wish to tackle the job with the help of an instruction book. It may be worth enrolling in an evening or day class so you can carry out repairs under supervision. Another option is to give the job to a skilled local carpenter or upholsterer. Although not cheap, the final cost may still work out less than buying the equivalent in good or mint condition.

upholstery

A new slipcover and a few tacks may be all that's required to bring a sofa or armchair back to life. However, if any springs are sticking through the underside or there is a serious stuffing deficiency, it will be a bigger, more complex job to put right. For dining chairs this can be reasonably straightforward, but for large sofas and armchairs, buy the book, take a class, or get it done professionally.

loose legs and joints

As long as there isn't too much damage to the leg ends or pieces to be glued,

fixing loose joints is a simple task. Casters can be replaced—look for old ones in secondhand stores. Seek advice on the best types of glue.

drawers

It isn't particularly easy to replace split or missing drawer bottoms, so think before you buy. Providing the frame is not damaged, a cleanup, some sanding down or planing, and candle wax applied to the runners will improve the fit of most drawers. Handles are easy to replace and can change an item's character as well.

wood, veneers, and laminates

Solid wood can be stripped, scrubbed, or sanded to bring out its original color and grain before rewaxing or oiling. While it is possible to repair damaged veneer, it is a tricky, skilled job. Old colored laminates are often chipped and can't be repaired, so you have to decide whether the damage is part of a piece's charm.

wash, wax, and oil

There are proprietary products, specially formulated for washing wood and valuable pieces, that remove dirt and discolored

wax; you would be wise to use them. If not, a warm solution of gentle detergent (eco-varieties are good) will suffice. Use a soft, long-bristled brush to get into nooks and crannies. For stubborn dirt and stains, use a scouring pad. Rinse off the soap and dry thoroughly with a cloth. Apply Danish or finishing oil or a good-quality wax polish to bare wood. If you plan to paint the wood, first apply a coat of primer. For painted surfaces, either seal the existing paint with a thin coat of wax or apply fresh paint directly on top of the clean surface.

strip

Old painted furniture can be full of charm, but beautiful wood should be liberated from suffocating coats of paint or varnish. Stripping is tricky and messy, as it involves the use of caustic chemicals, which are corrosive and give off unpleasant fumes. Be careful. Buy a good product, follow the instructions to the letter, and wear protective gloves and clothing and the correct type of mask. Don't rush the job. Don't try to remove the paint before it has properly softened, as this will only require more stripper to get all the paint off.

simple chair repairs

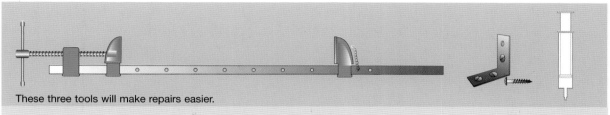

These three tools will make repairs easier.

You will need a clamp to keep all parts in position while the glue dries. Small right-angled metal brackets can be used to strengthen joins and frames as an alternative to glueing or to add extra support. A syringe is great for getting glue into nooks and crannies.

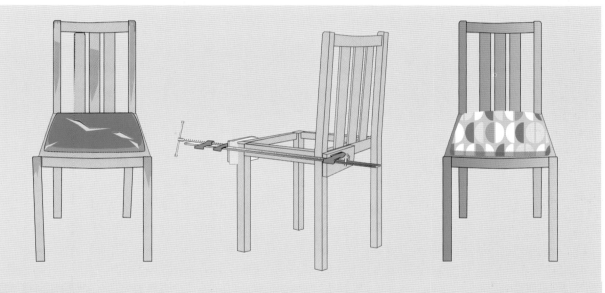

Chairs such as these are usually very cheap and plentiful, and as they are well made and robust, they can easily be rehabilitated. Take out the seat pad and clean down the frame, stripping off any varnish if necessary. Check all the joints and, if loose, glue them in place using a clamp. Use the clamp vertically when glueing joints on the top rail. Treat the repaired chair frame with oil or wax. Remove the existing seat cover, including as many of the old tacks as possible. Add more padding to the seat, if necessary, and cover with new upholstery fabric by pulling it over the frame and tacking into position underneath. Bear in mind that if you intend to sell on any item of furniture, all stuffing, padding, and upholstery fabrics must be flame retardant.

furniture finishing touch

waxes and oils

Applying wax or oil protects wood, gives it a better, mellower color, and revives older pieces. There are a confusing number of proprietary products for treating wood—which you choose will depend on the finish you require and the state of the wood you are treating. These products are either wax- or oil-based. Waxes dry to a hard finish and can be buffed to a shiny coating that keeps out dirt and protects against scratches. Oil soaks into the wood and gives a soft, matte finish. New softwood furniture is often finished with a coat of hard-wearing varnish to protect and color the wood. This coating is not very flattering and looks cheap. Rubbing with abrasive paper will break down this surface and allow oil to penetrate, giving the wood a subtler, more natural finish.

Danish or finishing oils

A thinnish liquid that is easy to apply with a brush or cloth, this kind of oil forms a water-resistant surface and prevents woods from drying out and splitting. Essential for treating new wooden worktops, oils should be reapplied at regular intervals to keep wood in good condition. Oils can also be used on wooden furniture, shelves, and built-in cabinets.

liquid waxes

When wax is dissolved in solvent, it is easier to apply. Most liquid waxes have a stain added—usually light, medium, or dark. Liquid waxes are useful for putting life back into dry wood and toning down or deepening its color. Some dry to a hard finish, so check on the tin.

beeswax polishes

The best furniture polish is made from beeswax, blended with solvent and perfumed with lavender or lemon. Go for the purest blend and avoid products containing silicone, as this forms a surface buildup that is difficult to remove.

wood stains

Choose from light yellow pine to almost-black ebony. Paler tones are safer, but dark stains can look sensational providing you apply them evenly, which can be tricky over large areas. Once applied, stains cannot be removed, so know what you are letting yourself in for.

age gracefully

There is a lot of reasonably priced new and secondhand reproduction furniture around, including tables, chairs, and some quite grand-looking beds. While the shapes and quality are fine, the finish is often crude, making the piece look less than elegant. However, with a bit of work, such a piece can be improved and rehabilitated. Remove hard varnished or gilded surfaces using abrasive paper, steel wool, and, if necessary, paint stripper. Use abrasive paper to smooth down and soften all sharp edges, including any decorative moldings. Wash thoroughly and allow to dry before applying wax or oil for a natural finish or a coat of primer before painting with an eggshell paint—creamy white or pastels look best.

varnishes

Use clear varnish for a finish that is hard-wearing and waterproof. There are many different types to choose from, but a matte finish is best. Many varnishes are polyurethane-based so will darken paint colours and add a yellowy tinge to white. To avoid this, use an acrylic varnish on a painted surface.

finishing school

These techniques can be used on all furniture, from small shelves to large armoires. The larger the item, the better the quality of finish needs to be, so brush up your technique before tackling any large-scale projects.

gloss

The shiny look went out of favor for a while, but this hard-wearing, solid-color finish is perfect for smartening up or adding character to plain pieces. Before painting, apply a primer to bare wood, and, in order to achieve an even color, use an undercoat (a coat of latex flat will do). Follow with two or more coats of gloss. Rub down between each coat using fine steel wool or abrasive paper. For an even finish, use vertical brushstrokes only.

latex flat

Besides being cheaper than gloss, latex flat is easier to use. Though not as robust as eggshell or gloss, it can be used on furniture if you seal the surface with either a clear varnish or wax polish. Beeswax polish gives a soft sheen finish, which will improve and harden with regular polishing. For good colors and finishes, use specialist paints.

specialist paints

There are some wonderful specialist paints around, many of which are based on traditional recipes and made from more natural ingredients. Not only do they have a color intensity, subtlety, and finish that is not possible with the more chemically based paints, they are also a healthier option. They are low in VOCs (volatile organic compounds). Water-based versions of eggshell and gloss are also available. Casein or buttermilk paints (based on the old milk paints) have a soft, chalky finish that, when used on furniture, will need to be finished with a coat of acrylic varnish (avoid polyurethane, as it will darken the color and make white look yellow). Eggshell gives a soft sheen, and dead flat oil paint has a dense matte finish.

crackle glaze

Products that give a crackle effect can be bought from craft supplies stores, specialist decorating supplies stores, and some home centers. Finishes vary from quite crude to very subtle. Application varies according to the brand, but the process involves painting the crackle glaze on top of paint, causing it to craze, and then rubbing on a darker color paint or wax to reveal the crackle lines. Use latex flat, as it goes on easily and dries quickly. Practice on scraps of wood first.

distressing

To achieve a worn look, apply a coat of paint, followed by another, different color on top; then, using fine steel wool, rub off some of the top coat along the edges and other areas of high wear. Alternatively, after the first coat of paint, rub the edges and patches with a wax candle to resist the second coat of paint. To give the appearance of several layers of old, chipped paint, continue the process using a different color each time.

If you are desperate to use some of the gorgeous papers around, why not paper the inside of a cabinet or wardrobe or use one to line your drawers?

You may be lucky enough to find a collection of splendid old wallpaper samples. The back of a closet door is the perfect place to stick them, as you can admire them without interfering with the rest of the decor.

paper pleasures

If "découpage" conjures up images of rosebuds and lampshades, think again. Forget cutting out small shapes and motifs; use sheets or lengths of paper in a bolder way. There are so many wonderful designs, patterns, and effects available in paper form, as wallpaper, giftwrap, and handmade and art and craft papers, it seems silly not to make the most of them. The découpage principle remains the same: stick on the paper using wallpaper paste or spray adhesive and cover with a protective coating of clear varnish. If you tire of it after a while, it is not too difficult to remove.

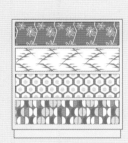

chest

Jazz up an inexpensive, plain wooden chest of drawers using different papers on each drawer front. If the paper isn't as wide as the drawers, you will have to join pieces, but don't worry too much about matching it exactly, as it will add to the crazy feel. If jazz isn't your style, try art or handmade papers.

wardrobe

There are some wonderful wallpapers around with huge motifs that can be cut out and stuck to a dull wardrobe to give it a lift. You may have a length left over from a serious wallpapering job or have found a bargain, but if not you could decide to buy a single roll. Or try asking for a sample.

door

There is no law that says doors have to be plain. If you want only a small amount of pattern in a room or you have only a limited amount of paper, the door is as good a place as any to make your statement. For an over-the-top, overall look, paper the walls as well, and watch the door disappear.

frugal fabrics

While we may be confident in choosing clothes that suit us and are comfortable, we often show less assurance when it comes to dressing our homes. Following the same fashion preferences and applying the same dress rules to your decor is likely to be more successful than getting hung up on interior fads. Look inside your closet and the glossy fashion magazines for inspiration.

textile style

The hardest thing about buying fabrics is what to choose. Sometimes a fabric will dictate an entire decorative scheme, but whatever its role, keep your mind on how it will fit in to the general scheme of things.

Fabrics provide the finish for an interior, giving it warmth and character. Depending on your requirements and preferences, textiles can be a barely noticeable presence or a striking main feature. Good-quality fabrics can be very expensive, but there is plenty of choice in the cheaper bracket, so thrift-conscious decorators still have several options.

You could choose to use a beautiful, pricey fabric but limit it to small quantities—a short ungathered curtain, a simple shade, a single chair cover, or an individual cushion. If you prefer a more opulent look, go for cheaper fabrics. Thrift shops and house clearance sales sometimes have great bargains from a bygone age ready for a comeback. Even if you can't use the item as it is, you may be able to cut it up and remake it into the perfect accessory for your room—maybe even a splendid pair of draperies.

How you use fabric, and how much you use, depends on your chosen style. For the pared-down look, plain and simple curtains and blinds or window panels in a color similar to the walls will blend into the background and won't spoil the clean lines.

Fabrics are an ideal means of adding decoration in the form of color and texture—brighten up your interior with either the latest designer patterns or pretty prints and chintzes. If you want to make a statement, add a touch of drama using a stunning color or bold print for draperies, throws, or a wall hanging. A length of fabric can work wonders in detracting attention from unattractive surroundings, disguising ugly furnishings, or hiding equipment, appliances, or a mess.

Your choice of fabric type will depend on its intended use. Covers for chairs, sofas, and footstools need to be made in a robust fabric in order to withstand normal wear and tear, plus any extra demands such as children, pets, or the accommodation of weary feet. Closely woven cottons and linens are ideal, as many are washable—a useful thrifty attribute.

If you buy new upholstery, the retailer will insist that the fabric conform to regulations related to fire risk, and it should have an appropriate certificate. This doesn't apply to homemade chair or sofa covers, but it might be a good idea to check the small print of your insurance policy just in case.

The notion of formal drapery fabrics has long gone out of the window—nowadays anything goes, so be imaginative. Cushions and throws provide the opportunity, and perhaps the inspiration, to do some sewing, so try your hand at patchwork, appliqué, or quilting. Don't forget beds, which can look smart and fashionable or downright sexy and alluring, dressed with a variety of cushions, quilts, bed skirts, covered headboards, and even curtains and canopies. Silk-lined walls may be a bit over the top, but you can hang fabric in the form of a wall hanging or large panel, or you could tack it to the wall as a more permanent feature.

fabric file

natural fibers

Solid-colored cottons and linens, including denim, are great for everything from upholstery to draperies and can usually be washed easily to keep them looking good.

textured weaves

Crunchy cotton and linen weaves allow you to add variety using texture.

wools

Wool tweed, suiting, and cashmere are chic but often require specialist cleaning.

traditional prints

Chintz and toile de Jouy look cozy in a traditional country-cottage way, while sprigged flowers have a fresh appeal. Provençal prints are bright and cheerful and often inexpensive.

luxury

Velvets, silks, and damasks add glamour when used for lavish draperies or throws.

bold prints

Let them stand out in a simple setting. If you are nervous of quantity, use them for just a cushion or a shade.

textile style cheapskate choice

cheap

Inexpensive cottons can be found in markets and the kind of stores found in the less elegant areas of town. In addition to pretty prints, there are dots, stripes, and ginghams and many dress fabrics, which tend to be cheaper anyway. Thrifty travelers will pick up Provençal prints in the South of France and other colorful cottons in Asia, Africa, and Latin America. Those who do not go abroad may find them in ethnic shops and markets in big cities.

basic

Plain cloth is inexpensive, but its simplicity makes it nonetheless appealing. Unbleached muslin is great but does shrink, so wash before sewing. Ticking has a pleasing crisp appearance, is hard-wearing, and is available in a variety of stripes. Denim is perfect, as it not only is hard-wearing but famously improves with age. And, just as jeans go with anything from a crisp white shirt to a sexy, silky top, so denim looks comfortable in any interior.

old

No thrifty shopping excursion would be complete without a trip to the secondhand store or a browse through a flea market. Thrift shops are a good source of seemingly outdated designs that only you and others in the know realize are, in fact, the latest thing. Bold fabrics from the 1960s and '70s, which even fairly recently wouldn't have been given houseroom, suddenly look perfect for brightening up a sterile space.

bed linens

Flat bed sheets can be bought quite cheaply and can be incorporated into curtains and covers. With new bed linen you get a lot of fabric for your money. New flat sheets are wider than fabric bought on the roll, they come ready stitched (you could unpick the sides and thread the top edge onto a pole), and are good as generous curtains. Pure cotton is best—if you use a synthetic version it might look too much like a sheet. If you particularly like the color and design of a duvet cover, you could use it as fabric.

remnants and scraps

Dive into the remnant bin in both the decorator and dress fabric departments for an opportunity to buy something that would otherwise be way beyond your means. It is an excuse to introduce a dash of something special by way of cushions, or chair covers or for use in patchwork or appliqué.

top trimmings

Fancy trimmings are expensive, especially when it takes several yards to trim draperies or a bedcover, but there are thrifty ways of brightening up or glamorizing the mundane.

make

While away a few relaxing hours making crochet flowers using up odd balls of yarn bought in sales or from thrift shops and market stalls.

Relive your childhood by winding wool around circles of cardboard to make perky pompoms.

Knit your own trims: books on knitting generally include a variety of lace edgings for use on home accessories.

sew

Add blanket stitch around the edges using a big needle and thick yarn in a contrasting or subtly similar color.

Bind edges with strips of printed fabric. Ideal for using up scraps, remnants, and small but fabulous pieces of vintage fabrics, including old clothes.

recycle

Salvage fringes, lace, buttons, ribbons, and even pockets from old clothes, bedspreads, linens, cushions, shawls, scarves, and lampshades.

dressing up and covering up

Good sofas and armchairs can be expensive. It's difficult to know what to do when the condition of your sofa cover deteriorates or the shape or color of your chair that looked perfect when you bought it suddenly doesn't live up to current expectations. New fitted slipcovers can also be costly, unless you make them yourself, but there is a way to freshen up sofas, chairs, and daybeds. Think "dressing up," rather than "covering up"—take the fashionable layered look as your inspiration, and use throws, rugs, and even scarves, shawls, and pashminas to mix colors and textures as you would clothes. Choose the style that suits you, as well as your interior.

The habit of throwing large bedspreads over unsightly sofas in a desperate attempt to hide or brighten them up is common, but however carefully they are draped and tucked in, they inevitably end up wrinkled and creased if you dare to sit down. Layering, using a variety of sizes and materials, works better, as it distracts and disguises, rather than attempting a complete cover-up.

smart

For a tailored look, choose smooth textures and subtle colors in cashmere, felted wool, fine weaves, and plain knits. Smarten up a scruffy sofa with collar and cuffs in crisp cotton or linen for a new take on antimacassars and arm protectors.

casual

Wrap up furniture in chunky knits, crochet, fleeces, sheepskins, tartan rugs, and the more subtle fake furs. Add cushions in knits, denim, cords and shaggy wools.

bohemian

You can always go hippy with Indian and African prints, plus any colorful, embroidered odds and ends, and maybe even a sheepskin.

eastern glamour

Create an aura of opulence with kilims, thin, Persian-style carpets, and pashminas. Add an Eastern influence with jewel-colored silk and a few tassels and fringes.

vamp

Drape fringed silk shawls over a sofa or, better still, a chaise longue. Wake up tired chairs with glamorous crushed velvet throws. Finish off with touches of silk, satin, and lace.

pretty

An excuse to indulge in pretty prints, chintzes, and cretonnes, as well as an opportunity to use odd lengths, remnants, and scraps of fabric to make patchwork throws, covers, and cushions. Provençal prints brighten up any dull chair, and sprigged flowers always look fresh. A crisp white embroidered or lace tablecloth makes a perfect antimacassar.

sew stylish cushions and throws

There is a definite movement toward "slow living," as a reaction against the fast, almost out-of-control pace of modern life. Many people are choosing to slow down and find time to take up creative pursuits. Indeed, crafts have undergone a renaissance, and some practitioners are earning a living from painting, drawing, potting, knitting, and sewing.

sew easy

This throw was made using two inexpensive fabrics, one printed and one solid colored. A very cheap, fleece blanket was sandwiched in between to give a quilted look, as well as extra warmth. A more quilted effect can be achieved with simple straight lines of stitching or, if you prefer, a more complex decorative pattern.

pretty alternative

Antique embroidered napkins and lacy doilies are charming and can often be picked up for next to nothing. Sew two napkins together to make a pretty cover for a small pillow or cushion, then stitch a lacy doily on top of the natural crunchy linen or starched cotton.

Craft work may not be the new salsa, but it can be a fascinating and satisfying pastime. Whether you choose delicate embroidery or wild knitting, it provides the opportunity to make anything from a napkin to a bedspread, using new or recycled remnants, and is great for anyone interested in making something beautiful that doesn't cost a fortune.

crochet revival

Crochet is very much in vogue, so old crocheted cushions and blankets are quickly snapped up in rumage sales and thrift shops. Picking up some yarn and a crochet hook yourself (or asking someone else to do it for you) is the next best thing. It's easy and fun and gives you an excuse to buy some of the fabulous new yarns now available.

prudent patchwork

Patchwork is popular, but the best can be pricey. Less than half a yard of fabric was enough to make these unusual cushion covers. Sew up simple pockets or sleeves in which to pop plain cushions. There's no need to to waste any fabric, as individual blooms can be cut from the scraps and appliquéd onto solid-colored fabric.

sew stylish chair flair

Fabrics have had a low profile in recent years, as the plain and bare modern style replaced the elaborate draperies, valances, and trimmings of the 1990s. Nowadays, fabric (along with knitting and crochet) is back and has brought with it a new appreciation of pattern, especially the prints from the middle decades of the last century. Patterned fabrics are creeping back onto chairs to brighten up the room, to disguise the horrors hidden beneath, or to add a little more comfort. A small amount of woven or knitted fabric can go a long way to cheer up a chair, especially if used with verve and imagination.

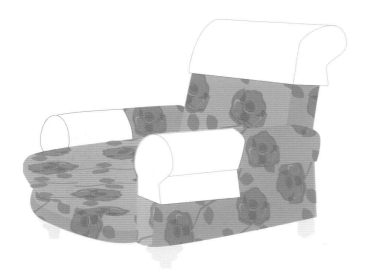

tailored style The backs and arms of armchairs are vulnerable to wear and dirt. This modern version of the antimacassar adds a crisp, clean set of "collar and cuffs" to protect a new chair or cover the grubbiest parts of an old one.

fashion item The fashion for ponchos comes and goes. When they are out of favor, why not make good use of them on a chair?

office wear Office chairs don't have to wear work clothes. Although they can be dressed to blend in with the surroundings, why not go for something unsuitable?

bobble hat A silly woolly hat will enliven a plain chair and anybody's day. Get knitting.

cover-all Making tie-on covers for this type of chair is relatively easy. They can be removed for washing or for a change of style.

two-piece Pop a simple slipcover over the chair back, and add a covered cushion to the seat. Depending on the fabric, you can turn an ordinary chair into a retro piece or something altogether more refined.

added comfort These fold-up chairs are a great invention, but the seat back can be uncomfortable. A small sewn pad, folded over and fixed with snaps makes a world of difference.

cover-up Cut a piece of fabric big enough to cover the seat, allowing a generous border and rounding off the front corners. Hem along the edges, and thread elastic through to make a semi-fitted cover.

sew stylish slipcovers

Upholstery is one of the biggest furnishing costs. Good-quality sofas and armchairs are expensive, but a worthwhile investment, as they are generously proportioned, more comfortable, and, most importantly, will last longer than cheaper alternatives. Those who choose wisely and opt for a classic shape will find it easy to fit old upholstery into new interior schemes, especially if the covers are in neutral, solid colors.

It is possible to find a bargain old sofa or armchair that is very well made but in need of re-covering. Whether you have bought to last or bagged a bargain, a new cover will be necessary at some time, to cover either worn and grubby patches or outdated patterns and colors. However, new slip covers don't come cheap and can cost as much as a new sofa, so do your sums and don't waste money if your furniture is structurally poor and the cushions and padding are saggy. Far better, in that case, to buy new and, if possible, buy something that will last.

custom-made

The fitted, tailored slipcover that snuggly hugs every curve and is finished with smart cording or kick pleats is a costly item. It can, however, be money well spent, as the end result is a sofa or armchair that looks new and will give several more years' good service. Of course, the cost depends on the fabric and whether you make the cover yourself or have it done professionally. If you are considering doing it yourself, you really need to understand how things fit together, as well as being a proficient

sewer. The cost of engaging a reputable professional (either an individual or a company) can be more expensive than the fabric, but will ensure a job well done.

The stretch covers often advertised extensively in the backs of magazines and colour supplements are (thankfully) no longer so popular, but many companies are now offering tailored slipcovers at a reasonable rate. These are a good-value option, provided you have standard-shaped sofas and chairs and are prepared to choose from the fabrics available.

loose

Technically, all slipcovers are loose, in that they can be removed, but a more casual, less-tailored cover is another option. Less complicated to make, loose slipcovers are a possible do-it-yourself option (although you still need good sewing skills), as simple, uncorded seams and a plain hemmed bottom edge are easier to cope with. This variation should also be cheaper to have made, as it involves less work.

baggy

The new kid on the slipcover block is the baggy cover, which ignores the structure

underneath in favor of a simplified slipcover made with fewer pieces and straighter lines. The look is in the spirit of Tuscan or Provençal farmhouses, with bare floors and rustic furnishings. While baggy slipcovers will never look smartly tailored, they can look chic if you use a plain white or neutral fabric. For anyone wishing to try making their own, instructions are given on the next page.

fabric choice

Covers need to withstand a fair amount of wear and tear, especially if your household includes children, pets, or couch potatoes. Good-quality, closely woven cotton and linen will wear well, natural fibers are comfortable, and if the fabric is machine-washable, so much the better. A lighter-weight fabric could be used for baggy covers, but don't expect it to last long. If choosing a pattern, bear in mind the problems of lining up and matching up, and allow extra fabric for this. Small designs will be fine, but stripes and geometric patterns look better if they line up and all go in the same direction. Big plaids and floral patterns also look best if they are matched, at least on the fronts of the arms.

simple chair cover

Slipcovers can be complicated to make, especially if the shape of your chair is curvy, rather than straight up and down. Getting something to fit all the forms takes time and skill, but fortunately a more casual cover is in vogue, which is a lot easier to make.

Ideally, upholstery fabrics should be hard-wearing, so a thicker close-weave material is usually recommended. For the novice do-it-yourself sewer, however, these fabrics are difficult to handle, and the seams too much for an ordinary domestic sewing machine to cope with. Using a lighter-weight fabric will be fine, as long as it isn't too flimsy. There are plenty of medium-weight cottons and linens around, both patterned and solid-colored, but don't choose anything that obviously frays easily, as the seams will be weak.

Unbleached muslin is a good upholstery option, as it is inexpensive but very robust, as are denim and ticking. It is always best to wash any fabric before cutting out as many of them shrink—after its first washing, your trendy baggy cover may end up with a more fitted shape than you anticipated.

This baggy cover is pared down to the simplest shapes, the minimum number of pieces, and not too many curves. It is relatively simple to make, but take care and time. Remember: measure twice, cut once !

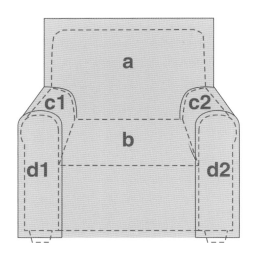

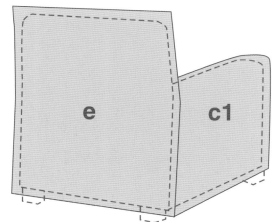

Use the diagrams above to calculate the amount of fabric needed. The best way to cut the pattern pieces is to lay the fabric, wrong side out, over the chair and mark with tailor's chalk. Cut out the pieces on a flat surface or in situ. Do not forget to add a seam allowance of approximately 1 inch on all sides.

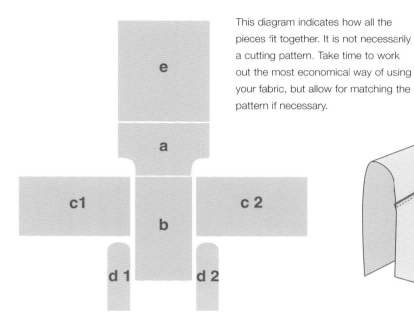

This diagram indicates how all the pieces fit together. It is not necessarily a cutting pattern. Take time to work out the most economical way of using your fabric, but allow for matching the pattern if necessary.

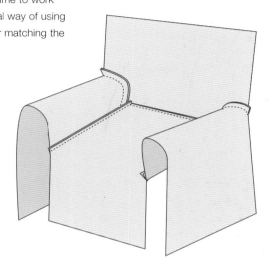

Stitch A to B along top straight edge. Place wrong side out on chair, and pin C1 and C2 to sides of B. Sew in place. Pin, baste, and stitch curved seam joining C1 and C2 to A.

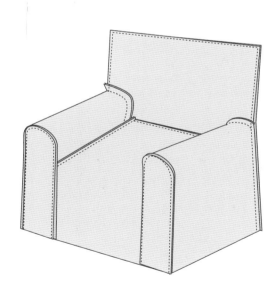

Place cover over chair. Pin and baste piece E to A across top and to C1 and C2 at sides. Pin and baste D1 and D2 to C1 and C2. Remove cover and stitch.

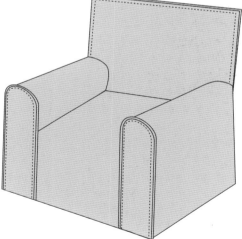

Turn cover right side out, and place over chair. Either leave it with simple seams or add a row of stitching on the right side, around back and arms, to add definition.

budget headboards

There is no shortage of stylish beds at bargain prices, and, although many of them look perfectly OK on their own, they can be made to look smart, special, or even sexy with a small budget plus a little imagination. Choosing from a wide selection of fabrics, bed linens, quilts, covers, and cushions, you can dress up a bed in a variety of styles from crisply prim to outrageously opulent.

Your bedroom is the one private place where you can indulge in a style that is more distinctly your own. Here you have the opportunity to use fabrics in a way that may not suit the rest of your home or those who share it with you. However, you don't have to go for the frilly and flowery look. You may prefer to take your inspiration from the cool, smart, luxury-hotel style, with the emphasis on plain but luxurious bed linens and calm, restful colors.

For a crisp look, use plain linens and cottons, such as denim and cord. For something completely different, use a piece of patchwork or vintage prints. For opulent luxury, go for heavy velvets or damasks, or for a smart, hip-hotel look, use woolen moleskin or smooth tweed. Keep an eye open for sales bargains and remnants in specialist shops, and the dressmaking and furnishing fabric departments of big stores, and scour antique markets and garage sales for old curtains, linens, and quilts.

Upgrade the humble box spring with a luxury padded headboard. The cost of the basic materials—a piece of particleboard, thick batting, and tacks—

is low, though the final cost depends on the fabric used. However, it does provide an opportunity to use a fabulous, and perhaps fabulously expensive, fabric that will infuse the whole room with its sumptuousness. The amount required would be less than would be needed for draperies; so you could go for an inexpensive window treatment and let the bed take center stage.

A padded headboard is relatively simple to make, using a piece of particleboard covered with fabric, with a layer of padding underneath for comfort. The size of the headboard should be a little wider than the bed and as high as you like. Fix it at mattress height, or, for a full-length version, at base board level. When calculating the amount of padding and fabric needed, allow for the size of the board plus at least 6 inches all the way around. Lightly sand any sharp, cut edges of the board to prevent damage to the fabric. Cover one side of the board with extra thick batting (available from notions departments) or fleece, securing it at the back with staples or small tacks. Next, cover the padding with the chosen fabric, using staples or large-headed

tacks. To hang it securely on the wall, use hidden hooks, set into the back.

A lightweight, ready-to-hang headboard can be made using an artist's canvas. Many art supplies dealers stock ready-made canvases in large sizes, though probably not the width of a double bed. However, they normally offer a made-to-measure service, and, considering the size, the price is very reasonable. Alternatively, you can buy artists' canvas by the yard and make your own frame using ready-cut stretchers that easily slot together. Stretching the canvas tightly and neatly requires care and a certain amount of skill, though, so you should tackle it only if you are good at that sort of thing. The final look is up to you and your artistic aspirations; you can leave the canvas blank, paint a picture yourself, or commission one from a friendly local artist.

5 bed ideas

For that casual, arty look, simply pin up a rectangle of fabric behind the bed. A piece of coarse linen looks suitably austere, but a scrap of velvet or damask (leave the frayed edges if you dare) adds a dash of unconventionality. For a smarter and more permanent look, sew around the edges, put eyelets along the top, and hang from hooks screwed into a batten fixed to the wall.

Plain bedsteads come cheap, but sometimes they are a little too neat and shiny. Soften them by draping a quilt over the headboard.

Layer your bed with throws, blankets, and bedspreads. Don't be afraid to mix the very expensive with the dirt cheap—an old embroidered tablecloth turns a cheap plain cotton bedspread into a vintage treasure.

Sex up a plain bed with silks and satins. Why not hang curtains from a pole screwed into the ceiling? Light, floaty ones are romantic, but damask or velvet will add history and warmth.

Gathered bed skirts can look a bit passé; new ones are tailored to hang straight. If you don't want to sew them, simply use a throw, sheet, blanket, or quilt thrown over the bed base underneath the mattress. Use as part of a layered look, mixing patterns, textures, and colors.

curtains etcetera

Curtain and drapery fashions come and go, but the recent enthusiasm for a pared-down look has led to more curtains being taken down than put up. However, naked windows are an acquired taste and are neither practical nor desirable when neighbors and passersby are close, or if your room temperature plummets when there is a gentle breeze. A room can seem unfinished and cold without curtains or draperies, but they can be discreet, distinct, or designer—whichever look takes your fancy.

straight up and down

Simple panels with little or no fullness, hung from plain poles or rails, are not only easy to make; they use the minimum amount of fabric. The very simplest (and perfect for the ultimate casual look) is a piece of unhemmed fabric hung from a bamboo cane.

opulent

Go all the way for swags and drapes in velvets, damasks, and even chintz. Frighteningly expensive if new, but look in sale rooms, secondhand stores and house clearance sales. Alternatively, use a very inexpensive fabric but use it generously and add tiebacks (cheap, colorful cords can be found in home centers) and perhaps the odd tassel.

lacy and floaty

Glass curtains and other sheers are making a comeback. Not only do they shield you from nosy neighbors; they also keep out the dust and dirt (and are much easier to clean than a blind). Gathered or hung in panels, the more interesting sheers make a statement. Go for old or new lace, translucent cotton weaves, or glamorous chiffon and sari fabrics.

pretty plain

Cotton or linen, printed or solid-colored, slightly gathered on a rod or a simple pole. Works well in bedrooms, where you can indulge in pretty florals. Look in street markets, where you can often buy printed dress cottons very cheaply.

thermal

Keep out winter winds (and reduce the heating bills) with quilted, padded, or thick lined draperies. Put a layer of batting in between two different fabrics, and quilt either with a sewing machine or by a few knotted stitches here and there.

blind or shade

The price of ready-made blinds and shades is impressively low. Wooden or metal venetian blinds always look smart and modern and complement most styles. Roller shades are neat and roll out of sight during the day. On a large window, use two or three narrow ones in a row. White roller shades are perfect for the minimal look at minimal cost. Pleated paper shades are another thrifty option.

These draperies are a trimmed-down version of a much-loved old pair, which were fuller and had pleated headings. The old pleater heading tape was removed and replaced with a flat strip of buckrom. New linings were made from inexpensive lightweight fleece, which protects against drafts without making the draperies heavy.

curtains something different

Bare windows may be fashionable—and the ultimate thrifty solution—but unless you are lucky enough not to be overlooked, they are not an option. The bare look can also feel cold, whereas a window treatment can complement the decor and complete the picture, as well as screening out drafts and prying eyes.

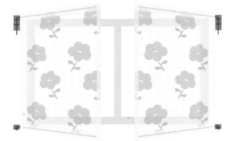

swing arm rods Panels hung on swing arm rods require a relatively small amount of fabric, as there are no gathers.

Use a basic fabric, and keep costs right down or indulge in a small amount of a more expensive material.

café continental A piece of pretty fabric attached to a length of wire with clothespins is all you need.

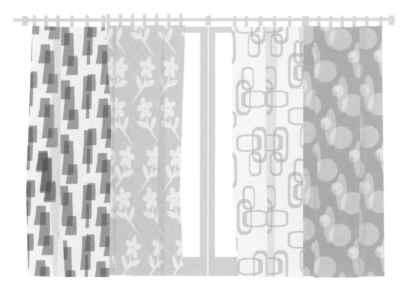

mix and match You may not have enough precious vintage fabric to cover an entire window, so take the opportunity to display a whole collection of different designs. Don't be afraid to mix and match.

lace panel A single lace panel could be new or old, need not fit exactly, and can be dyed for extra impact.

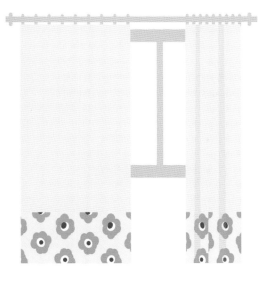

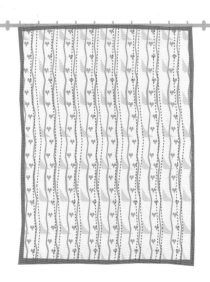

bold borders Liven up an otherwise plain pair of curtains with a border of something special or extravagant.

flimsy curtain Gather a filmy fabric skirt to a thicker fabric top, strong enough to take the hardware.

quilted cozy Quilts look pretty and keep you cozy in bed. They fulfil similar functions when used as a curtain.

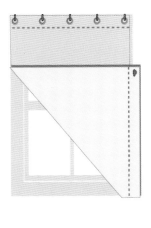

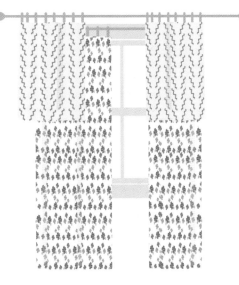

dhurries Inexpensive dhurries make great window coverings. Hang from a pole and make a feature of the fringe.

fold-back panels Hang a plain panel from simple hooks; fold it back to reveal a contrasting lining.

layer curtains Size doesn't always matter, especially if you are prepared to mix, match, and use your imagination.

curtains/draperies measurements

As there is now a more relaxed attitude to curtain and drapery widths and lengths, measuring for them does not have to be so crucially precise. The thrifty bonus is that the fashion for a simpler look with minimal fullness means that less fabric is required.

If you choose a patterned fabric with an obvious horizontal design, it is best to match the design across both panels; otherwise it will look odd. Don't forget to buy extra fabric—a lot of stores will state the pattern repeat measurement, which will help you to calculate how much fabric you need. Similarly, if you are joining more than one width of fabric to make a single panel, it will look better if you match the pattern along the seam.

If you don't want the bother of making the whole thing, go for ready-made curtains or draperies. Some are great value and can be personalized with borders, appliquéd or crocheted flowers, patchwork panels, fringe, buttons, and bows.

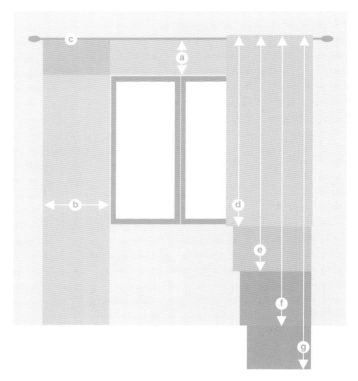

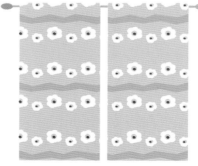

a height at which you hang the rod—ideally, this should be in position before the finished length is determined
b allow enough room for the fabric to clear the window
c drapery/curtain rod
d sill length
e cropped
f floor length
g extra-long

simple draperies

If you can sew straight lines, you can make curtains or even draperies. A sewing machine is useful, but if you don't have one, then sew by hand—it is easy and very therapeutic. Fortunately, modern window treatments are plain, rather than fussy, so there is no need to tussle with the intricacies and expense of fancy headings and pleats.

To make a simple drapery panel, turn in approximately $5/8-3/4$ inch of fabric along both sides, and then fold in again so that no raw edges are visible (an iron makes this easier). Pin and baste in place, then stitch along the inside edge. Do the same along the top edge, but fold over up to 3 inches of fabric to provide space and extra strength for heading tape, curtain hooks, or rings. Stitch the folded side seam.

If you want the curtain to reach to an exact position, such as the top of the windowsill or the floor, turn the bottom edge last, and work out the turn up with the curtains hung in place. This edge is normally hand-hemmed, as the fabric hangs better, but you can machine-stitch the bottom hem if you prefer.

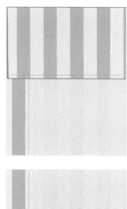

The extra weight of lined draperies makes them hang better. You can make a detachable lining with touch-and-close tape.

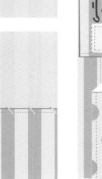
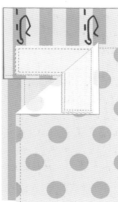

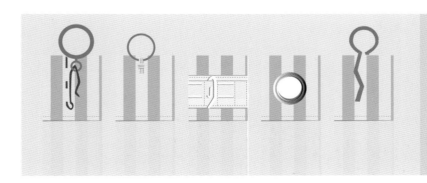

The range of hooks and rings for hanging draperies and curtains is wide. Whether your choose sew-in rings, clip-on hooks, or eyelets depends on the weight of your draperies and choice of rod or pole. Eyelets do not require any hooks, as they thread directly onto a pole. Just make sure they fit!

thrifty fixtures and fittings

bamboo canes

Inexpensive and available in a range of lengths from garden centers.

thumbtacks

Pin fabric to the window frame with thumbtacks for an impromptu curtain.

wooden dowels

Thin dowels will support lightweight curtains, while the biggest will hold heavier ones, with the right supports.

piping

Put up copper and plastic piping using plumbers' hardware.

bulldog clips

Good for no-fuss curtain hanging. Thread or clip onto string, cord, or wire.

wire

Steel wire, strung between eyelet hooks and held taut by tensioners, looks smart, minimal, and modern.

plastic-coated wire

An easy way to hang sheer fabrics.

make-do window dressing

If you don't want the bother of sewing, take advantage of the numerous lengths of fabric available with ready-finished edges in the form of tablecloths, sheets, "throws" as well as off-the-rack curtains and draperies. But if you are an exponent of shabby chic or the spontaneous style of interior, don't be afraid to use fabrics in their raw, unfinished states.

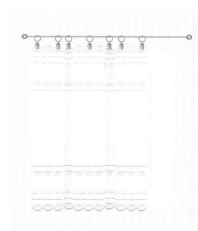

tablecloths

Tablecloths come in a wide range of fabrics, colors, and designs. They come with ready-sewn edges, so they can be put to use right away. Smaller lightweight cloths can be hung from clips or sewn-on curtain rings. Crisp, white embroidered tablecloths look pretty in bedrooms and bathrooms.

lightweight linings

If you have opted for a lightweight fabric curtain but feel the need for a little more substance, use another lightweight fabric as lining. This is useful in children's rooms, as the double-thickness curtains will block out more light. You could use two sets of inexpensive, ready-made curtains sewn together.

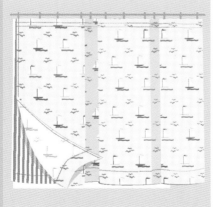

casual drapes

A generous length of fabric draped over a pole looks dramatic, with a hint of grandeur. Anything can be used. An old linen sheet is perfect, but old velvets and damasks add a dash of opulence.

good housekeeping fabric care

Looking after fabrics prolongs their life as well as keeping them looking good. We all frequently wash our bed linens, but often neglect throws, covers, and window treatments, as they aren't so easy to deal with. Dust eventually turns into dirt, and it is surprising how much finds its way onto fabrics. So get into the habit of regularly vacuuming your upholstery and any heavy draperies. Natural fibers are easy to look after, but anything special, such as velvet, damask, silk, or wool, should be professionally cleaned, unless stated otherwise by the manufacturer.

For cottons, linens, and colourfast dyes, the best cleaning method is machine washing with a good detergent. If you don't want to risk the super-sized machines at the launderette for large items, it may be better to get curtains and slipcovers laundered professionally, especially if the fabric is expensive or the colors are likely to run.

Modern detergents cope easily with general dirt and occasional stains. Some biological varieties can be harsh, so stick to the non-bios and those formulated for colored fabrics. For very fine fabrics, such as voiles, embroideries, and loose weaves, hand washing in tepid or cold water with gentle soap is advisable. Washing or cleaning instructions are usually provided when you buy new fabric, throws, and cushion covers, but in the absence of such information, test a small corner first. Anything with deep colors is best washed separately at a low temperature or, for non-colorfast dyes, in cold water.

whiter than white

Old linens are often gray or yellow but usually whiten after a few hot washes. Bed linens and table linens will have been washed several times and therefore won't shrink—anything that doesn't survive a hot wash with detergent would not be much use anyway. Any yellow tinge can be removed by soaking in a solution of $3/4$ ounce chlorine bleach to 5 quarts water. Alternatively, try soaking in a bowl of warm water with two denture cleaning tablets dissolved in it. Remove mildew stains by rubbing with lemon juice and salt and leaving out in the sunshine.

ironing

You may be pleased to know that for bed linens and table linens, the creased look is in. Screwed up like a rag will not do, however; it has to be an orderly crease. As soon as you take the washing out of the machine, shake all items and pull into shape. When dry, fold neatly and smooth down by hand. Except for large or expensive items, sending ironing to a laundry or getting someone else to do it are not very thrifty options. For unwieldy amounts of fabric or awkward shapes, such as slipcovers, you can iron them in situ using a steamer, formerly used by professionals but now available for domestic use.

upholstery

There are plenty of proprietary products for cleaning upholstery yourself, but don't attempt it unless you know what you are doing—the foam, padding, or feathers underneath may react badly to the wrong cleaning method. Look for a care label, and use appropriate products accordingly. If in doubt, get it done professionally.

professional cleaning

For luxury fabrics, professional cleaning is the best option. Dry cleaning is the usual method; and although it's expensive, the items do get pressed as well—something that can be tricky to do yourself.

Steam cleaning by a professional company is recommended for upholstery with fixed covers. The cleaner normally does the job in your home.

repairing

Unsightly, threadbare patches reduce the life of sofas ad chairs. When you buy an upholstered piece of furniture, ask for a scrap of the fabric, and use this for patching, if necessary. If this is too conspicuous, you may need to resort to slipcovers or reupholstering.

save energy

Being thrifty is not only about spending less; it also involves questioning and reassessing your priorities and addressing the wider implications of how you choose to spend your money. For some people, cutting down on consumption is a necessity, while for others it offers an opportunity to adopt a different attitude to life, whether approached from a personal or a global perspective.

the "re-" issue

The mantra of energy conservation and eco-consideration is "Reduce, reuse, and recycle." There are many more "re-" issues that benefit not only our environment but also our personal well-being.

It's not a bad idea to stop and re-evaluate your life from time to time. Personal circumstances change, as do ambitions and aspirations, and in today's competitive market there is no certainty of economic stability. Many people are choosing to downshift—sometimes of necessity, in order to cope with changes in work situations, relationships, marriage, children, or retirement—while others are making a conscious decision to improve their quality of life by reducing the stress caused by trying to keep up with financial commitments.

The dictionary definition of thrift refers to frugality and economical management, which may sound rather worthy. However, it can be a liberating experience to care less for material possessions and more for your health, wealth, and happiness. Adopting a holistic approach to "re-" issues involves taking into account the state of your mind as well as that of your bank balance. Reconsider where you live, how you live, and what you live for. Think positively and imaginatively—readjusting your aspirations to bring them into line

with your income doesn't have to mean exchanging designer labels and meals out for sackcloth and gruel. Taking a look at your finances, how you use them, and where you could save is a worthwhile exercise; and even if you are not prepared to make any sacrifices, the exercise may spur you on to earning more money!

A thrifty approach is not just about cutting down and doesn't always have to mean change. Thrift is more about reconsidering your priorities, changing direction, and, perhaps, thinking laterally. If you are a fashion freak, for example, it isn't necessary to forgo the latest trends. Following fashion can be enormous fun, but it also contributes to a vibrant, forward-looking, forward-thinking society. Design is no longer regarded simply as an ornament, but is acknowledged as an industry that uses innovation and invention to create better, and often cheaper, products.

Thrift is currently very fashionable, and there is no longer any stigma attached to buying secondhand—though it has put the prices up, which makes it even more important to stay ahead of the game.

So being fashionable can be good for you, your pocket, and the world. Pursuing a thrifty lifestyle is very 'à la mode'.

10 Rs

reduce
Think before you spend your money, reduce your intake, and use fewer resources. Pause for thought before you buy, and consider whether you will benefit from the purchase. Buy what you need rather than what you want.

revive
Reawaken old passions by reviving past interests in hobbies, sports, artistic activities, and other pastimes. Anything from knitting to kite flying, jogging to jiving can bring you pleasure, and the cost needn't be high.

reorganize
Save time, money, and your temper by reorganizing your home, your possessions, and your habits. Make sure there is somewhere to put everything, and that anything that is used frequently is kept to hand.

reuse
Plastic and paper bags can often be reused. Keep them neatly sorted in a kitchen or utility room cabinet. Instead of disposables, buy washable cotton diapers, handkerchiefs, and dishcloths that consume fewer raw materials.

reinvent
Besides putting old furniture to new uses and turning old clothes and fabrics into cushion covers and patchwork quilts, think big and reinvent the way you use your home to make it more practical, pleasing, and energy efficient.

reclaim
Old floorboards, bricks, and window frames can be reused, so either recycle or sell them on. Reclaimed materials, which are often better quality and nicer looking than new equivalents, are sometimes cheaper.

recycle
Glass, newspaper, plastic, cans, and other items can be given a new lease on life. Various organizations (check the Internet) redistribute computers, electrical appliances, furniture, clothes, and books to good causes.

refresh and reinvigorate
Tired homes need little more than a good clean and a coat of paint to reawaken your interest. Instead of splurging on something new, reinvigorate a room by moving the furniture around.

relax
Have a night in with a good book, video/DVD, or cozy chat. Eating out is fun but expensive. For the cost of a main course, feast on bread, cheese, cold meats, and pastry, which don't require any cooking.

rethink
Reevaluate the way you live your life, from your diet and dress to your home life and work life. Instead of shopping during lunch, visit museums or galleries, where you can often view the permanent collections for free.

conserve, create, and support

We are constantly exhorted to "Save the Planet." In truth, the planet will survive, whatever we throw at it, which is more than can be said for the human race. Conservation has become a global issue. Whatever your views or understanding, it is widely agreed that reducing energy consumption makes good thrift sense.

power and fuel

Turn off appliances completely; the standby state uses a surprising amount of electricity. Don't waste energy boiling more water than you need—fill the kettle with only what you require. Energy Star-rated washing appliances are inherently energy efficient, but use them efficiently, too, by ensuring there is always a full load and using a low-temperature wash cycle and, if available, an economy wash. Transportation is the biggest user of energy, so keep car journeys to essential ones; and, where possible, walk, cycle, or take the bus.

heat

Look at the big picture, and make sure your home is well insulated. Attic insulation is easy to put in place. Wall insulation is not so straightforward, but if you are buying or renovating a home, it is worth considering. Cellulose and materials made from recycled paper and wool are eco-options. Make sure that your thermostat is a programmable or automatic setback type, which will automatically regulate the amount of heat or air conditionaing produced. Prices vary according to the sophistication and flexibility of the system, but all can produce significant energy savings. You

may like bare windows, but an enormous amount of heat is lost through glass and badly fitting frames. Thick and generous draperies that cover the whole window frame will not only keep in the heat but also make a room feel warmer. Apply weatherstripping to windows and doors. Some v-channel fitted to the sashes of double-hung windows will prevent drafts; casement windows can be made more air-tight with strips of seld-adhesive foam, which can also be used on the side and top edges of external doors. Apply a door sweep to the lower edge.

light

Save energy and switch off unnecessary lights, and don't leave lights on in empty rooms. However, a low level of light can be depressing and not good for the eyes (and for safety make sure that steps or stairs are well lit), so use a good task light for reading, working, and cooking. Fit energy-saving bulbs where possible.

water

All toilets now sold in the U.S. must be of the low-flow type, using only 1.6 gallons per flush, as opposed to 3.5 gallons or more in older models. New showers, too, are designed to use less water. You can do your part to conserve water by taking a

shower instead of a bath and by simple measures such as not leaving the water running while you brush your teeth. If you have a garden, catch the rainwater for watering plants by rerouting the downspout to a large plastic or metal tank or garbage can. You could install a "rain harvester" on the downpipe, which filters the water and diverts it to a butt or storage tank for use for the washing machine and flushing loos as well as the garden.

health

Thrift doesn't always mean choosing the cheapest. Where health is concerned, penny-pinching is not appropriate. And with worries about allergies, harmful chemical pollutants and VOCs (volatile organic compounds), it makes sense to pay a little more for the healthy option. Go for "natural" paints with ingredients made from renewable natural minerals and earth and mineral pigments, as they allow the wall to breathe, avoiding condensation problems and are therefore better for both your home and your body. Healthy versions of plaster, flooring materials, and fiberboards are also available, and demand and legislation are helping to bring the prices down. Walking, running, and cycling are healthy activities and much cheaper than joining a gym.

solar power

There is satisfaction and money to be gained if you produce even a tiny amount of the power you consume. The statistics regarding the cost efficiency of solar water heaters are confusing, but any reduction in bills is welcome, and it is silly to let all that sunlight go to waste. Installation is costly and therefore a long-term investment, although since we are living in a time of energy crises, a solar heating system may well increase the resale value of your house.

wind power

Wind farms, another source of renewable energy, have become familiar sights in some parts of Europe and are gradually beginning to appear in the U.S. It will probably be a long time before many households can obtain their energy from wind farms, but small wind turbines, suited for domestic use, are available

food

Grow your own vegetables. If you are not lucky enough to have a garden, you can still grow tomatoes on a balcony, herbs on a windowsill, potatoes in a trash can, zucchini and scarlet runner beans in large pots. If you do have a garden, recycle waste to make compost.

fair trade

Don't just recycle your trash; buy products made from recycled materials, including glass, paper, and plastic. Buy lumber from renewable resources—look for the FSC mark of the World Wildlife Fund's Forest Stewardship Council. Buy Fair Trade items to ensure that producers get the best price for their hard work.

stay local

Cut transportation costs (your own plus those of retail industries) by buying local produce where possible. Support local stores and markets. Join community schemes and activities such as car pools.

money

All the foregoing can save you money. Simply not spending saves even more, but in today's retail environment, spending can be addictive. No one is suggesting going without, but remind yourself to buy what you "need" rather than "want." Being thrifty can give personal satisfaction and reduce anxiety, as well as overdrafts.

easy energy savers

energy-efficient bulbs

They use 75 percent less energy and last up to 12 times longer than normal bulbs. They are more expensive, so buy in bulk via mail order to save money. The range of sizes available is now very wide, so there's no excuse not to use them.

Energy Star-rated electrical appliances

Choose items bearing the Energy Star logo, including fridges, freezers, washing machines, and dishwashers. They are more efficient in the amount of power and water that they use.

condensing boiler

The initial installation cost is higher than a standard boiler, but they cut energy consumption by up to 4 percent.

wind-up radio

The clockwork radio was originally invented for use in remote areas of the world where no power was available, but the fact that they don't need batteries gives them added eco-cred. Look for wind-up cell phone chargers, too.

solar-powered garden lighting

Solar panels may be out of the question for your home, but consider installing small versions to run your garden lights. Don't expect a high level of illumination, but who wants that in a garden anyway?

cheap
organizers

bulldog clips
Organize anything from bills to photos using a selection of bulldog clips in different sizes and colors. Either hang them on hooks or string behind a door or display them as a feature.

plastic folders
Keep papers safe and orderly by filing them in clearly labeled plastic folders, which can be kept neatly in a filing cabinet, drawer, or large box. If you can't cope with frequent filing, put everything in a "pending" folder so things don't go astray.

ring binders
Instead of keeping an unruly pile of papers, punch holes in everything and put them in ring binders, where they can be quickly filed and can't fall out and get lost. File papers by subject in different-colored binders on a shelf that can be easily accessed.

bags and baskets
If you can't resist buying bags and baskets, use them for storage. Hang them on a row of hooks where you can access the contents easily, or line them up on a shelf to make a display.

magazine files
Ideal for filing away papers, as they are easy to pop things into. Buy one for each category—bills, pending, filing—or for each household or family member.

get organized

If you are organized, you will save both time and money, and life will be less tense if everything from important papers to sports gear can be found in the right place at the right time. You don't have to be an organization freak, but a little discipline and a few storage products will result in a well-organized house that is more relaxed and efficient—and probably looks nicer, too.

Carelessly stored possessions are at risk of being lost or damaged, as well as mislaid, and items such as clothes, utensils, tools, and treasures will last longer if they are properly stored and cared for. Something as simple as a hook near the door for your keys or a large ceramic bowl for tossing bills in can save time, and tempers, when next you need to leave the house or pay your dues.

Organize your kitchen so that frequently used utensils and gadgets are at hand and food is stored in visible and appetizing order. Keep tools together, either in a specially-made toolbox or hanging on hooks or a rack, where you can find them and they won't get damaged.

Rethink your rubbish disposal, and recycle as much as possible. Make it easier for yourself and any others in the household with a system of receptacles for each recyclable material. A set of different-colored bins will look cheerful in a kitchen, or outside in the yard, but if space is limited, use large baskets, which will look good in a hallway or living room. State your eco-virtues with a row of brightly colored, labeled bags available from mail-order companies (or make your own), and save valuable floor space by hanging them from sturdy hooks screwed to the wall.

If you have a garden, a compost heap is a must, and there are plenty of containers and systems, for both indoors and out, to ensure the production of good compost, rather than a soggy, smelly heap.

Clothes will last longer if they are looked after by being hung up and put them away (which can also save on washing, as clothes left lying around are often put in the washing machine when they are not really dirty). You will save time finding and choosing what to wear if you organize them into groups by colour or type of use.

paperwork

Being able to find important papers or documents can also save you from potential delays, trouble, and possible fines. Make sure all legal documents are filed away in an accessible and safe place. It's a good idea to keep passports, certificates, etc., in a metal, fireproof box.

Don't hide bills away in the hope that they will pay themselves; keep them on a bulldog clip in an obvious place to remind you to deal with them. If possible always pay on time to avoid penalties or extra interest. Automatic transfer is a convenient way of paying bills. Many companies and organizations offer discount incentives if you pay by this method, so take advantage of it wherever possible.

reaping the benefits

What you get out of being thrifty will depend on how widely you apply the philosophy. There is bound to be some benefit or saving, be it small enough to allow an extra treat or big enough to change your whole life.

new look

If you follow the advice in this book, you may achieve a newly stylish home that not only looks better but feels and works better, too. The same principles applied to your clothes could turn you into a more together fashionista.

new interests

Giving up expensive nights out is one way of saving money, but you don't have to stay in. For the cost of one night out on the town, you could enrol at a local evening class to learn just about anything, from I.T. to tango, fitness to yoga. Alternatively, go jogging, which is free, and spend the money saved on pursuing those latent talents in pottery, painting, or textiles classes. Now is the time to take up dancing. Discos are dull compared to jive, tango, or tap. Why not indulge in some ballroom dancing (and go to dressmaking classes to make your own glamorous evening dress)? Because it is never too late to learn, use some of

your hard-saved cash to buy that musical instrument you have hankered for—and get playing.

Local societies can be fun. The price of one theater ticket could well be more than a whole year's subscription to the local amateur dramatic society, where you can indulge your thespian ambitions on the stage or behind the scenes. The whole experience could result in much more drama than you would get in an evening on Broadway.

If you enjoy enjoy gardening, rip up the decking and gravel and replace it with a vegetable patch. It can supply you with produce throughout the year, while providing a pleasurable way to fill evenings and weekends.

new life

The smallest change in lifestyle can lead to a big, life-changing decision. Many people are downshifting from stressful, high-paid jobs to part-time or lower-paid employment, which offers more free time and satisfaction in place of money. Some are also moving from expensive properties, either to smaller spaces in the town, which offer more in the way of local facilities and cut down on travel, or to bigger spaces with, perhaps, a garden, in a cheaper area. Others are

opting out and taking on the challenge of a new, alternative life in the countryside or abroad.

Nowadays, few people expect to remain in one job or career, and retraining can bring about a different direction or better prospects. Pursuing a thrifty lifestyle can free up money to pay for this training and could result in a larger or more regular income, or just a nicer life.

New interests can lead to new business opportunities. You may find that your prowess at pottery propels you into a career as an artist or shop-owner, or an I.T. course provides you with enough expertise to start a small home business.

new attitude

Eschewing consumerism in favor of lower outgoings should bring peace of mind and freedom from some of the pressures of modern-day life. It can also raise awareness of the wider world, including issues of the environment, the economy, the need to conserve resources, and the need for sustainability. In addition, you may become more aware of the needs and problems of others, all of which might change your attitude to the world in general and make you feel you want to do your bit, either as a voluntary worker, as an eco-campaigner, or by working for a charity. This could involve work abroad, spending a weekend reclaiming a meadow, or spending a few hours a week working as a volunteer at a local hospital.

something special

Spending money isn't a sin; in fact, it keeps the economy going; so why not

spend money saved on the mundane on something beautiful, such as a work of art, or something special, such as a fantastic vacation of a lifetime? However, some of the best things in life are free, and a little extra cash or extra time will enable you to appreciate more fully the landscape, a blue sky, or the opportunity to relax and enjoy a better life.

index

accessories 15, 17, 29; bathroom 90, 93
advertisements 49
antiques 19, 48, 52
appliances: electrical 55, 134, 135; gas 55, 75
armchairs 24, 25, 50, 52, 53, 58, 59; cleaning 42, 128; covering arms and backs 112; cushions 17; layering with throws 109; loose covers 25, 104, 113, 115, 116-17; repairing/patching 128; reupholstering 94
Art Deco chair 53
Arts and Crafts furniture 52, 53
artworks 17, 19; see also pictures
auctions 48

bags and baskets (for storage) 70, 71, 83, 136, 137
bathrooms: accessories 90, 93; floors 90, 93; lighting 90; mirrors 93; painting 90; showers 93; tiling 90, 93; walls 90, 93; ventilation 93
bedrooms 26, 28, 35, 40, 41; boudoirs 31
beds 40, 50, 104, 119; headboards 104, 118, 119; linen/sheets 51, 106, 128; valances 119; see also bedspreads
bedspreads 25, 31, 51, 119
beeswax polishes 97, 98
benches, garden 65
bills, paying 137
blankets 17, 25, 51
bleach 44
blinds 7, 23, 26, 120; cleaning 42
bohemian style 17, 31
boilers, condensing 135
bookcases 25, 36, 57, 63

box cushions 61
boxes 60, 70, 71
brooms/brushes 44
building works 74
bulbs, energy-efficient 134, 135
bulldog clips 136, 137; for curtains 126
bureaux 51

café curtains 122
café furniture 59
calico 106
candles, scented 45
carboot sales 49
carpets 6-7, 23, 26, 31, 76, 77; cleaning 42
casein paints 98
castors 23; replacing 94
chairs: covering 113; dining 39, 59; hanging on walls 80; repairing 94, 95; see also armchairs; furniture
chandeliers 55, 68
charity shops 29, 49, 104
chests 20, 36, 49, 70
chests of drawers 36, 41; wallpapering 101
china 38
chipboard flooring 77
cleaning 24, 26, 42, 43, 94, 128; tools for 44
clothes, organising 137; see also wardrobes
collections 18, 80
colour schemes 15, 18, 23, 26, 34
compost heaps 137
concrete floors 76, 93
conservatories 35
cookers 55, 82
cottons 104, 105, 106, 120; cleaning 128
crackle glaze 98
crochet 25, 111
cupboards 22, 28, 35, 36, 49, 71, 75; built-in 71; Georgian

52, 53; kitchen 85, 86, 87; lighting for 68; small 31, 50, 63; wallpapering 100; see also wardrobes
curtains 7, 23, 25, 31, 104, 120, 121, 122-3, 134; café 122; cleaning 42, 128; draped 127; fixtures and fittings for 125, 126; kitchen 83; linings for 127; making 125; measuring up for 124; net 120; portiere 122; tablecloths as 127; thermal 120; see also fabrics
cushions 7, 15, 17, 22, 24, 104; box 61; covers for 110, 111

Danish oil 94, 97
decoupage 101
denim 106
deodorisers, room 45
desks 49, 65; bureaux 51
detergents 44
dhurries 31, 123
dining furniture 39, 59, 88
dinner services 38
distempers 98
distressed furniture 24, 98
divans 61, 118
doors 34, 75, 76; draughtproofing 134; frames see woodwork; handles and knobs 50; in kitchens 85; wallpapering 101
downlighters 68
drapes 127
draught excluders 134
drawers: handles for 85; lining 100; repairing 94
dressers 41, 53
dressing tables 31, 41, 51
driftwood shelving 63
dust sheets 43, 44
dusters/dusting 42, 43, 44

eco cleaning 44

Edwardiana 51
eggshell paint 79, 98
electrical appliances 55, 134, 135
electrics 74, 75
emulsion paint 79, 98

fabrics 7, 20, 31, 57, 104, 105, 106; cleaning 42, 128; ironing 128; prints 31, 105, 112; remnants/scraps 106; trimmings 107; see also cottons; linens; wall hangings
feather dusters 44
filing cabinets 49, 65
fish tanks 17
flea markets 48
flooring 6-7, 13, 23, 24, 26, 34, 74, 75, 76, 134; bathroom 93; chipboard 77; cleaning 42, 43, 76; concrete 76, 93; laminated 77, 93; painting boards 23, 36, 77; recycling boards 133; stripping boards 77; tiled 77, 93; see also carpets
flowers/plants 17, 20, 45
folders, plastic 136
frames, picture 51, 67
French windows 34-5, 75
fuel, conserving 134
furniture 12, 15, 24, 25, 29, 56, 57; antique 19, 52; buying secondhand 39, 50, 51-3, 55; café 59; cleaning and polishing 42, 43, 44, 94; distressing 98; garden 25, 65; and harmony 20; leather 17, 25; modernist 23, 52, 58; moving 133; office 49, 41; painting 20, 24, 31, 36, 37, 94, 97, 98; recycling 41; repairing 94, 95; and scale 20; staining 97; stripping 94; waxing and oiling 94, 97; varnishing 97;

see also specific items

garden furniture 25, 65
garden lighting, solar-powered 135
gas appliances 75
Georgian style 29, 52, 53
gloss paint 36, 37, 79, 98
gluing chairs 94, 95

hall stands 50
hallways 34
hampers (for storage) 70
handles, door 50; kitchen 85
health and safety 75, 134
heating 55, 75, 134
hooks (in kitchens) 83

insulation 75, 77; loft 134
internet shopping 49
ironing 128

jumble sales 49
junk shops 49

khelims 31
kitchens 29, 34, 71, 82, 83, 88, 137; dressers 41, 53; equipment 50; handles and knobs 85; unfitted 86-7; worktops 82, 83
knobs, door 50; kitchen 85

laminated flooring 77, 93
lamps 38, 50, 55, 59, 68; clip-on 60
leather 17, 25
lights/lighting 23, 26, 34-5, 55, 61, 75, 134; in bathrooms 90; downlighters 68; feature 68; garden 135; pendant 53, 61, 68; spot 68; task 68; wall 68; see also bulbs; lamps
linens 51, 105, 106; cleaning 128
linings, curtain 127

lockers 87
loft conversions 35
loft insulation 134
loose covers see armchairs

magazine files 136
maps (for walls) 80
markets 48
minimalism 12, 22
mirrors 19, 29, 51, 93
modernism 22, 23, 52
money, saving 133, 135, 137, 138
mops 44

net curtains 120

office furniture 49, 51, 65
oils, Danish/finishing 94, 97
organisers 136, 137

paints 74, 79, 98; for floors 76, 77; stripping 94
paperwork, organising 136, 137
patchwork 25, 111
pendant lights 53, 61, 68
picture frames 51, 67
pictures 17, 19, 25, 67; lighting 68
plastering 74
plumbing 74, 75
polishes, wax 94, 97, 98
portiere rods 122
power, conserving 134
primer (paint) 79, 97, 98

quilts 123

radiators 55, 75, 134
radios, wind-up 135
ranges 55
recycling 41, 132, 133, 137
refrigerators 55, 82
retro furniture 52
ring binders 136
rugs and mats 23, 24

sales, buying in 57
sales rooms, auction 48
salvage yards 48-9
saris 31
scale 20, 23
scents, natural 45
scourers 44
second-hand, buying 24, 48-9, 50, 51-3, 55
'shabby chic' 24
sheds, garden 35
sheets, bed 51, 106, 128
shelving 25, 36, 62-3, 65, 75, 80; concealed 71, 83; lights for 68; for pictures 67
shopping 12, 13, 56-7, 133, 135; internet 49; see also second-hand, buying
showers 93, 134
sideboards 39
skips, raiding 49
smoke alarms 75
sofas 15, 20, 29, 53, 56, 59, 61; covering with throws 17, 109; covers for 24, 104, 105; cushions 17, 24; repairing 94, 128
solar power 134-5
sponges 44
stains, wood 97
stairs, using space under 35
steam cleaning 128
stencilling 31, 79
stepladders 44
storage 22, 23, 35, 49, 53, 59, 60, 70, 71; see also cupboards; shelving
stripping paint 94
suitcases (for storage) 70
swap shops 49

tables 24, 31, 36, 39, 49, 51, 61, 88
tea sets 38
textiles see fabrics
thermal curtains 120
throws 7, 15, 17, 31, 51, 104;

layering with 17, 61, 109, 119; making 110
ticking 106
tiles: bathroom 50, 90, 93; cleaning 42;ff floor 75, 77, 93; renovating 76, 90
transport costs 134, 135
trimmings 107

upholstery 104; cleaning 17, 44, 128; repairing 94

vacuum cleaners 42, 44
valances 1129
varnishes, wood 97, 98
vegetables, growing 135, 138
veneer, damaged 94
ventilation 45
Victoriana 51

wallhangings 31, 80, 104
wallpapers 24, 50, 75, 79; bathroom 90, 93; on doors and furniture 100, 101
walls 13, 24, 74, 75, 76; cleaning 42; creative coverings 80; knocking down 34; painting 34, 36, 37, 42, 79; see also wallpapers
wardrobes 36, 41, 51, 71; wallpapering 100, 101
washing machines 134
water consumption 134
waxes, wood 94, 97
wind power 135
windows 23, 34, 42, 75, 76; frames see woodwork
woodwork 52, 75, 76; cleaning 24, 42; painting 79
woodworm 55, 76
worktops, kitchen 63, 82, 83

Zen interiors 26

author's acknowledgments

Many thanks to my excellent fellow team members: Mary, the wonderfully fastidious art director, and Lisa, the perfect editor, who are both enthusiastic and fully paid-up members of the thrift club. Thanks also to Jane O'Shea for going with the idea.

publisher's acknowledgments

The publisher has made every effort to trace the copyright holders, architects, and designers featured in this book. We apologize in advance for any unintentional omission and would be pleased to insert the appropriate acknowledgment in any subsequent edition.

2–10 Graham Atkins Hughes; 13 James Mortimer/*The World of Interiors*; 14 Graham Atkins Hughes; 16 Hotze Eisma; 18–21 Graham Atkins Hughes; 25 Uli Schade/*Elle Decoration*; 27 Hotze Eisma/Taverne Agence/*Elle Decoration*; 28–32 Graham Atkins Hughes; 37 Hotze Eisma; 38–54 Graham Atkins Hughes; 58 Ray Main/Mainstream; 64–72 Graham Atkins Hughes; 78 Antony Crolla/*The World of Interiors*; 81 James Mortimer/*The World of Interiors*; 83–91 Graham Atkins Hughes; 92 Hotze Eisma; 96 Graham Atkins Hughes; 99 David Hiscock/Robert Montgomery & Partners; 100 Luke White/Interior Archive; 102–111 Graham Atkins Hughes; 114 Hotze Eisma; 119–121 Graham Atkins Hughes; 126 Bernard Touillon/*The World of Interiors*; 129–136 Graham Atkins Hughes.